**New Directions for
Community Colleges**

Arthur M. Cohen
EDITOR-IN-CHIEF

Richard L. Wagoner
ASSOCIATE EDITOR

Gabriel Jones
MANAGING EDITOR

Occupational Outlook for Community College Students

Richard M. Romano
Hirschel Kasper
EDITORS

Number 146 • Summer 2009
Jossey-Bass
San Francisco

OCCUPATIONAL OUTLOOK FOR COMMUNITY COLLEGE STUDENTS
Richard M. Romano, Hirschel Kasper (ed.)
New Directions for Community Colleges, no. 146

Arthur M. Cohen, Editor-in-Chief
Richard L. Wagoner, Associate Editor
Gabriel Jones, Managing Editor

NEW DIRECTIONS FOR COMMUNITY COLLEGES (ISSN 0194-3081, electronic ISSN 1536-0733) is part of The Jossey-Bass Higher and Adult Education Series and is published quarterly by Wiley Subscription Services, Inc., A Wiley Company, at Jossey-Bass, 989 Market Street, San Francisco, California 94103-1741. Periodicals Postage Paid at San Francisco, California, and at additional mailing offices. POSTMASTER: Send address changes to New Directions for Community Colleges, Jossey-Bass, 989 Market Street, San Francisco, California 94103-1741.

SUBSCRIPTIONS cost $98.00 for individuals and $251.00 for institutions, agencies, and libraries in the United States. Prices subject to change.

EDITORIAL CORRESPONDENCE should be sent to the Editor-in-Chief, Arthur M. Cohen, at the Graduate School of Education and Information Studies, University of California, Box 951521, Los Angeles, California 90095-1521. All manuscripts receive anonymous reviews by external referees.

New Directions for Community Colleges is indexed in CIJE: Current Index to Journals in Education (ERIC), Contents Pages in Education (T&F), Current Abstracts (EBSCO), Ed/Net (Simpson Communications), Education Index/Abstracts (H. W. Wilson), Educational Research Abstracts Online (T&F), ERIC Database (Education Resources Information Center), and Resources in Education (ERIC).

Microfilm copies of issues and articles are available in 16mm and 35mm, as well as microfiche in 105mm, through University Microfilms Inc., 300 North Zeeb Road, Ann Arbor, Michigan 48106-1346.

CONTENTS

EDITORS' NOTES

A common assessment of a community college lies in how easily its students obtain good jobs that are related to their course of study. Yet in a world buffeted by the forces of changing technology and globalism, surprisingly little has been written about the outlook for graduates of the occupational and technical programs that are so much a part of the community college mission.

This volume focuses on the trends in the labor markets most common to community college programming and thereby will assist community college leaders in thinking about the future. Edited by two economists, it brings that perspective to bear on the forces shaping those markets.

The volume is divided into two major parts. Chapters One through Three, in the first part, deal with the broader forces in the economy that have an impact on labor markets: the supply and demand for labor, technological change and globalism, the impact of increased credentialing, and the changing skill requirements of the domestic labor market. The chapters in the second part take these broad themes into more specific occupational clusters such as business and the health sciences. Included is a case study of how well the California community colleges have responded to the changing demands for workers in their local labor markets. A chapter on the changing nature of transfer programs completes the volume.

Since this volume has an economic focus, the first chapter, by Hirschel Kasper, provides a review of the basic forces at work in the labor market with particular reference to the community college. A number of the ideas introduced in this chapter are picked up in subsequent ones. In the second chapter, Richard M. Romano and Donald A. Dellow discuss the role that technological change and globalization have on job markets. Historically these forces have both destroyed jobs and created new ones.

In Chapter Three, Anthony P. Carnevale, Jeff Strohl, and Nicole Smith examine the impact of increased credentialing on the workforce and the connection between education and earnings. They argue that postsecondary education has become the arbiter of economic opportunity in the United States and raise concerns that if community colleges become strapped for revenue, they may be forced to abandon the nontraditional students they were created to serve.

Chapter Four begins the second part of the volume. In it, Dixie Sommers of the U.S. Bureau of Labor Statistics (BLS) explains how labor market projections are made and the risks involved in making them. From the myriad data collected by the BLS, she breaks out those jobs that require as their most important pathway either an associate degree or at least some postsecondary training. Labor market projections for these jobs are then provided through the year 2016. These projections and other BLS information were

NEW DIRECTIONS FOR COMMUNITY COLLEGES, no. 146, Summer 2009 © 2009 Wiley Periodicals, Inc.
Published online in Wiley InterScience (www.interscience.wiley.com) • DOI: 10.1002/cc.360

provided to the authors of the next four chapters and served as a basis of their discussions of specific occupational clusters.

In Chapter Five Janell Lang discusses the outlook in the fastest-growing sector, the health sciences. In Chapter Six Robert Walker looks at business and related fields, in Chapter Seven Peggie Weeks discusses the outlook in engineering technology occupations, and in Chapter Eight Gregory Talley and Susan Korsgren review the employment projections in the protective services field. Finally, in Chapter Nine, Michelle Van Noy and James Jacobs round out the picture by looking at noncredit workforce development programs.

Community colleges pride themselves on the flexibility and speed with which they respond to the needs of local employers. In Chapter Ten, Duane E. Leigh and Andrew M. Gill present a new approach for evaluating just how well they do this. Applying their method to the California community college system, they find uneven but generally positive results.

Although this volume covers major clusters of the vocational and technical programs that are typically offered by community colleges, it does not attempt to cover all such programs or explore the jobs that transfer students will hold once they obtain a two-year or a four-year degree. However, since transfer programs enroll such a large number of students and often have an occupational orientation, we touch on that mission in the last chapter, by Barbara K. Townsend. In it, she explores the newest mission of the community college, the granting of the bachelor's degree. As the previous chapters have pointed out, many of the high-wage jobs of the future will require a bachelor's degree or higher. In a number of states, the pressure for producing more bachelor's degree graduates for certain occupations is so great that states have granted some community colleges the right to do so. Whether this new mission will change the character and direction of the community college remains an open question.

Since this volume was written, the unemployment rate in the U.S. has almost doubled and the world economy has gone into a sharp cyclical decline. None of these short-run problems would cause us to change the long-run projections presented here. Once labor markets stabilize, we will return to the underlying long-run trends depicted in the chapters that follow. In the meantime though, community college enrollments, both full- and part-time, will accelerate in transfer as well as the vocational programs.

Richard M. Romano
Hirschel Kasper
Editors

RICHARD M. ROMANO is the director of the Institute for Community College Research at Broome Community College in Binghamton, New York, and a research associate at the Institute for Community Development and the Cornell Higher Education Research Institute at Cornell University.

HIRSCHEL KASPER is professor of economics at Oberlin College.

NEW DIRECTIONS FOR COMMUNITY COLLEGES • DOI: 10.1002/cc

1

This chapter provides some basic economic tools to help describe how labor markets work to enable employers and community college students to reach each other to secure productive jobs.

The Economics of Community College Labor Markets: A Primer

Hirschel Kasper

The community college has many roles and constituents: academic, professional, and vocational. Its curriculum may be distinguished from that of other institutions of higher education by its many courses designed to enhance students' immediate career opportunities, especially with nearby employers. This chapter, however, is less concerned with the specifics of these colleges' curricula and more concerned with the general principles governing the labor markets that their students will enter. Thus, it focuses almost exclusively on the job markets for community college students and the basics of labor market economics: the availability of jobs and the wages and salaries for those jobs, with attention to the elementary forces of supply and demand.

Labor Markets

The vocational success of community college students depends largely on the job opportunities that become available (what economists term *demand*) and the number and skills of other applicants for the same positions (termed *supply*). All else being equal, the larger the number of job opportunities, the more likely each student is to be successful in finding what he or she wants; similarly, the greater the number of competitors looking for the same positions, the more difficult it is for each to obtain the desired job.

Demand. Jobs that employers seek to fill are an end result of the decisions of the customers who use the employers' products and services. In

New Directions for Community Colleges, no. 146, Summer 2009 © 2009 Wiley Periodicals, Inc.
Published online in Wiley InterScience (www.interscience.wiley.com) • DOI: 10.1002/cc.361

other words, the demand for labor is a derived one: it is derived from the demand for the products that labor produces. Should there be a change in the demand for those products and services, the demand for workers will necessarily change. As a result, workers are always concerned about how changes in the markets for goods and services affect their job security. New technology almost always requires some new skills, even as it can leave some skills obsolete. If society wants community colleges to provide those new skills, the college curriculum and its faculty must be flexible but must also be able to distinguish between being responsive to new and necessary requirements and mere temporary opportunities. Start-up costs for some programs may run in excess of a half-million dollars.

The demand for labor depends primarily on two factors: how much workers produce and how much the sale of their production adds to the firm's total revenue. In competitive markets, the higher the price of the product or service, the more valuable the job done by the worker and the greater the demand for those workers. When customers are willing to pay a lot for a product or service, employers are willing to hire more workers. In that way, the price of the product can serve as a signal about what society wants. And if the markets are sufficiently competitive, employers will respond by increasing their demands for labor.

One force that has lowered the prices of some goods and services in recent years is the increased competition arising from the globalization of production. Globalization, like any increase in product competition, makes the demand for the affected workers more sensitive to wage costs. To the extent that the prices of American-made goods have fallen, the demand has inevitably fallen for the workers who make those products. This increased competition has led to lower wages in the United States for jobs that are susceptible to competition from abroad and to higher wages for jobs that require greater skills and education or merely personal contact. For example, as the increased competition from Japanese auto manufacturers reduced the demand for production workers at General Motors, it raised the demand for workers to sell and maintain the Japanese cars. In the past few years, a widening in the disparity of both skills and education has worked against any noticeable gain in the average earnings of U.S. workers and, just as worrisome, added to the rising inequality of income.

Workers' productivity depends not only on the skills they bring to the job, but also on the other resources, such as the capital equipment they use to produce the goods and the technology of production. In some situations, capital complements labor and makes workers more productive, just as a taller ladder helps apple pickers reach more apples or a blackboard helps an instructor teach students. In other situations, capital substitutes for labor, so fewer workers are required for the same rate of output.

Similarly, improvements in technology ordinarily make workers more productive; cell phones and computers, for example, have made it easier for workers to communicate and coordinate their activities. Improvements in technology can reduce the demand for some workers while increasing it for others. There is little demand today for workers who can repair typewriters or sell encyclopedias.

The number of workers employed in a particular occupation is also influenced by the wage rate. At high wages, fewer are employed than at a low wage, other things equal. Higher wages for autoworkers cause employers to use more robots, transfer jobs to countries where wage are lower, or demand wage concessions from their auto part suppliers.

Supply. From the workers' standpoint, the better the compensation (their wages plus benefits), the more attractive the occupation, other things being equal. Ordinarily, wages guide students' choices, so high wages and available openings for accountants attract more students into accounting programs, while low wages in other occupations reduce those enrollments. A community college education enables students to raise and broaden the skills they can offer to alternative employers.

Two-year public colleges especially attempt to respond quickly to changing requirements and labor market opportunities by starting new programs or expanding others in high demand. When they do so, the supply of workers seeking jobs in those occupations increases.

Should colleges and their graduates mistakenly flood the market with nurses, say, or accountants, wages in those occupations tend to decline, unless those low wages encourage many workers to seek employment elsewhere. And anything that makes it harder or more expensive to move into an occupation will tend to reduce the supply of workers in that field and raise wages. Thus, if nursing associations or other health policymakers raise the requirement for an R.N. to a minimum of a bachelor's degree, the supply of nurses will decrease, thereby increasing the wages of the both current and new nurses. One might justify the increased credentialing for nurses in terms of the increased skills necessary to do the job. In some occupations, though, the restriction on supply and its effect on raising wages may be the prime reason for requiring new credentials.

Shortages. Ordinarily there are shortages of workers in some labor markets and surpluses in others, but these imbalances seldom last. When there are continuing shortages of workers, employers often elect to raise wages to attract new workers into their employment or expand their usual labor markets for recruitment. If employers cannot obtain the number and quality of workers they want, they may train the workers at hand themselves or ask the local community college to do it. Workers who are flexible and mobile can take advantage of these different opportunities. By the same token, when jobs are scarce in a particular field, some qualified workers usually enlarge their search area, thereby reducing the observed surplus.

When we look at the U.S. economy as a whole, we find that the demand for workers increased roughly as fast as did supply, including that from immigration, so that over the past quarter-century, the average wage, adjusted for inflation, has remained roughly the same. The average employee's total compensation, however, including the hard-to-measure benefits, has increased. More workers are employed today than twenty years ago (146 million in 2007 versus 112 million in 1987), but also a larger proportion of the adult population is employed today than twenty years ago (63.0 percent compared to 61.5 percent). The jobs are certainly different, with fewer workers in manufacturing and agriculture and many more in health care and education. Continuously changing job opportunities and requirements are the prime reasons that so much emphasis is placed on basic transferable skills and flexibility. What is termed progress is not without personal and financial cost, but those costs can be reduced by providing the necessary basic skills and appropriate public policies.

The Hiring Decision

In competitive markets where resources are scarce, an employer's decision to hire someone is based on what it will cost to do so compared with the additional revenue, technically called the marginal revenue product, that the new employee is expected to bring into the enterprise. A hospital-based physician, no less than a carpenter, is expected to earn her keep, recognizing that measuring one's marginal revenue product is much more difficult in some situations (for example, when people work in teams) than in others. Labor market economists postulate that in the long run and assuming a reasonable amount of competition, the wages paid to workers reflect their productivity. In the long run, changes in workers' productivity are closely linked to changes in wages, adjusted for inflation. Productivity in turn reflects the skills and attributes that employees bring to the market (technically called their human capital), as well as the physical capital (such as machinery) that workers can use. A worker will be more productive if she knows how to use Microsoft Office, but if the software is not available to her, she cannot be as productive as she could be. Human capital is increased by gaining experience and investing in education. From the viewpoint of the student and the public purse, this investment costs money, but if it is successful, it generates a return over and above its costs, often expressed as a percentage return on the investment.

Human Capital and Rates of Return

Economists often regard the decision of a high school graduate about whether to attend, and thereafter to seek a two-year degree, at a community college as if it were an investment in one's own human capital. Such a decision not only involves the payment of tuition fees and expenses of commuting, but any forgone earnings from students who ordinarily would have worked instead of attending college.

Set against those immediate costs are the possibility for higher wages and better jobs in the long term. The U.S. Census Bureau reported that the average annual earnings of adults who earned an A.A. degree was just under $38,000 in 2005, nearly 30 percent more than the average of $29,448 earned by the workers with only a high school diploma (Scrivener, 2008). Kane and Rouse (1995, 1999) report that calculations of the rate of return to such costs show that for the average two-year graduate, the earnings are far in excess of the costs, ranging from an annual gain of 10 percent to as much as 27 percent per year, depending on the field of study, time period, and location of the colleges. Some of that gain is the result of significantly lower unemployment rates for community college graduates compared to those with only a high school diploma. Interestingly, Leigh and Gill (1997) find that the economic returns to adults who return to community college for a further certification or a formal degree are just as large as those who continued their education straight through from high school.

Research by Kane and Rouse (1999) indicates that community colleges appear to provide larger rates of return for women than for men, perhaps, as they suggest, because of the high value of the nursing degrees the colleges offer. As discussed in Chapter Five of this volume, nursing and the health science professions in general are expected to offer more new jobs over the next decade for community college students than almost any other field. Kane and Rouse (1999) also find that the value of the two-year degree is greater than the value of each of the two years together, suggesting a financial reward to completing the degree. This difference is sometimes pejoratively termed "credentialing" or "signaling," but it may simply enable employers to distinguish those who have proven they have the difficult-to-observe ability to complete a task. It should be noted, however, that only a minority of those students who enroll in a community college persevere long enough to receive a two-year degree. And because of work commitments, family responsibilities, or academic preparation, it typically takes more than two years to complete a "two-year" degree. (For additional studies, see Grubb, 1999.)

Student Choices

In a dynamic economy, a student's choice of college major and subsequent occupation can be influenced by the relative earnings expected from that occupation.

Relative Earnings. Kasper (2008), for example, reports that the proportion of four-year graduates who majored in economics from 1975 to 2003 is negatively correlated with the proportion who majored in biology; more important, the relative proportions mirrored the annual changes in the relative annual earnings of the professionals in those two fields over the twenty-five-year period. Arcidiacono (2004) also found that students' choices of fields to study were determined in part by the relative earnings across the fields. While it is unclear how students learn about the relative earnings of various careers, it is likely that community college students observe enough to gain a workable idea about the relative earnings of jobs in their local areas. Part-time or full-time students who currently work in the field no doubt already have an understanding of the situation.

Although there are no reliable estimates of the importance of relative earnings in students' choice of fields, it should be noted that community college students increasingly seek employment beyond the geographical area of their colleges, so the relevant current data are not easily accessible. Furthermore, the typical person changes careers half a dozen times during a working life, thereby loosening any tie between one's expected earnings while in college and actual lifetime earnings.

Other Dimensions. Relative earnings have proven to be an important influence on a student's choice of occupation, but other dimensions of a job also exert an influence. Whether the work is done inside (such as office work) or out (mail delivery), or whether the workers need to work separately or in a team, can be positive or negative factors depending on the views of each individual employee. An attribute that one employee may regard as positive, such as work "autonomy," may be a negative for another who would view the same condition as "lonely." In the market, the first worker may be pleased to have that kind of a job, but the second employee may require a wage premium to accept the "lonely" job, so the wage paid must compensate the worker for all of the worker's net economic advantages.

Certainly it is impossible to know all the attributes of a position or of an employee until one has worked for a while. That is one reason that so many workers who decide to quit their jobs are those who have been employed only recently: an important element of the job, or the employee, was unexpectedly disappointing.

Wages are usually the easiest job dimension to change, and changing wages and the wage structure, such as from salary to commission, can make the jobs more or less interesting to workers but also more or less costly to the employers who decide whether to hire them. Depending on the job, community college graduates may be paid an hourly or weekly wage, while others may receive an annual salary with no provision for overtime premium wages. In general, the more education a graduate has, the more likely the pay will be a fixed salary. Graduates who have a two-year degree are more likely to be paid an hourly wage than those who have a four-year bachelor's degree. Some employers offer quite high starting salaries to attract more applicants than they expect to hire and train in order to choose among them. Thus, as students begin to think about courses to take at community college, they may also consider the relative attractiveness of alternative jobs, taking current and future wages into account as one factor.

Further Considerations

The Bureau of Labor Statistics projections of the growth of jobs used in this volume are the most transparent and useful that are widely accessible, but they are not immune to thoughtful criticism (see Stekler and Thomas, 2005). In a consideration of long-term trends in job opportunities for community college students, for instance, two problems stand out as significant challenges for both the college and its students.

First, most of the easily accessible long-term estimates of forthcoming job opportunities describe the situation for the country as a whole, not for the specific local labor market ordinarily served by any given community college. The national projections are based on estimates of normal job turnover rates by industry and occupation for the country, expected changes in technology and prices, and expert opinion. Those projections may well be accurate for the average college but still not very helpful for any specific institution in the light of its local circumstances. For example, the estimate of the U.S. Bureau of Labor Statistics (2008–2009) that employment of home health and home care aides will grow by more than seventy thousand workers in the decade starting in 2006 may not translate into very many jobs for communities with little use for such services. From the community college perspective, the number of new jobs depends importantly on the size, age, and wealth of the population in the labor market area that it serves.

Second, many colleges have at least an intuitive knowledge of local trends in jobs, but local conditions can change unexpectedly. The local employment requirements are more subject to unexpected change than the country as a whole, so the community college curriculum may have difficulty remaining in step with local needs. Consequently colleges may be better off developing more general courses that can strengthen students' skills and give them the vocational flexibility should local conditions change or they decide to look beyond the local area.

In conclusion, this chapter has concentrated on the elementary principles that govern the community college labor market so that the reader may understand the broader economic forces operating over long periods of time. Some rather simple campus actions would seem to follow from this analysis. These include the following:

- The shift to wider labor markets and the instability of employment make it that much more important that campus leaders pay attention to not only to local but also national and global trends.
- Faculty as well as administrators should be encouraged to participate in local and national groups that will connect them to employers and keep them informed about employment opportunities. Colleges should facilitate the sharing of this information.

- Colleges should develop procedures to demonstrate to students the relation between their courses and alternative career possibilities to raise their program completion rates.

References

Arcidiacono, P. "Ability Sorting and the Returns to College Major." *Journal of Econometrics,* 2004, *121,* 343–375.

Grubb, N. W. *The Economic Benefits of Sub-Baccalaureate Education: Results from National Studies.* New York: Teachers College, Columbia University, June 1999.

Kane, T. J., and Rouse, C. "Labor Market Returns to Two- and Four-Year College." *American Economic Review,* 1995, *85*(3), 600–614.

Kane, T. J., and Rouse, C. E. "The Community College: Educating Students at the Margin Between College and Work." *Journal of Economic Perspectives,* 1999, *13*(1), 63–84.

Kasper, H. "Sources of Economics Majors: More Biology, Less Business." *Southern Economic Journal,* 2008, *75*(2), 457–472.

Leigh, D. E., and Gill, A. M. "Labor Market Returns to Community Colleges: Evidence for Returning Adults." *Journal of Human Resources,* 1997, *32*(2), 334–353.

Scrivener, S. "Improving Individual Success for Community-College Students." *Focus,* 2008, *26*(1), 7–13.

Stekler, H. O., and Thomas, R. "Evaluating BLS Labor Force, Employment, and Occupation Projections for 2000." *Monthly Labor Review,* July 2005, pp. 46–56.

U.S. Bureau of Labor Statistics. *Occupational Outlook Handbook.* 2008–2009. Accessed February 28, 2008, at http://www.bls.gov/oco/print/oco2003.htm.

HIRSCHEL KASPER *is professor of economics at Oberlin College.*

NEW DIRECTIONS FOR COMMUNITY COLLEGES • DOI: 10.1002/cc

2

Globalization and technological change will continue to eliminate some jobs and create others, generating a need for skilled, flexible workers with a global perspective.

Technological Change, Globalization, and the Community College

Richard M. Romano, Donald A. Dellow

In early nineteenth-century England, workers now known as Luddites roamed the countryside destroying machinery that they saw as creating unemployment and upsetting their traditional way of life. They were, of course, right: the growing mechanization of production, what we would now call technological change, and the expanding volume of trade ushered in the industrial revolution and disrupted traditional patterns of life. The neo-Luddite movement of today has similar worries and is evidenced by the antiglobalization sentiments that produced riots in the late twentieth and early twenty-first centuries in Seattle, Paris, and London.

A clear lesson from history is that changes in technology and increased trade both destroy jobs and create new ones, thereby creating great opportunity and wealth for some and unemployment and hard times for others. On balance, however, economists are uniform in their belief that technological change benefits not only producers and consumers but, in the long run, workers as well. This is because, along with increased trade and competition, it shifts domestic resources, including labor, away from low-productivity (and therefore low-wage) industries to higher-productivity (and therefore high-wage) industries. This is what happened as the U.S. economy shifted from an agricultural to a manufacturing to a service economy. Over the past two hundred years, this process of economic development has raised average incomes and greatly improved living standards.

This chapter explores the impact of trade and technological change on employment within a modern context, with a view toward the job prospects

NEW DIRECTIONS FOR COMMUNITY COLLEGES, no. 146, Summer 2009 © 2009 Wiley Periodicals, Inc.
Published online in Wiley InterScience (www.interscience.wiley.com) • DOI: 10.1002/cc.362

for students enrolled in the programs typically offered at the community college.

Technological Change and Employment

As an economic phenomenon, technological change, or what is normally thought of as technological progress, takes two major forms. First, it may be an innovation that creates new production techniques or new products and services that did not exist before. Second, by changing the mix of inputs, for example, substituting machines for labor, it can lower the cost of production and the price of existing products or services.

In the first instance, the demand for the labor that produces or uses the new goods and services will increase, but the demand for labor associated with older or now-obsolete goods and services will decrease. Looking at recent history, it is easy to see how innovation has created whole new industries and spurred the demand for those who can work in or use these new technologies. If the nature of the technological change allows the automation of certain processes, then some workers will lose their jobs, but additional employment will be created as the prices of goods and services falls, freeing up purchasing power for further spending. Furthermore, automation allows productivity to rise and rewards workers still employed in a given industry with higher wages. Thus, we see over long periods of time the substitution of machines for labor in agriculture and manufacturing, and increasingly in service industries, resulting in increases in output with fewer workers per unit of output but each earning higher wages.

Since its peak in the early 1980s, the United States has lost about 5 million manufacturing jobs. Even during the period of recent economic expansion from 2001 to 2007, 1.8 million were cut. Although this trend will continue, it is premature to declare an end to the manufacturing era. The United States still leads the world in manufacturing output, but its workforce is now smaller and more skilled. U.S. Bureau of Labor Statistics projections reaching out to 2016 show manufacturing output, adjusted for inflation, rising at a 2.4 percent annual rate but employment, over the same period, falling at an annual average rate of 1.1 percent. This would be a further loss of 1.5 million jobs (Franklin, 2007).

Much of the loss in manufacturing jobs in recent years has been due to the widespread introduction of information technology and related technological change, which resulted in the rapid growth of productivity. The jobs that have been hit the hardest in the past twenty-five years, however, are those requiring low skills. According to a 2006 study done by the Federal Reserve Bank of New York, the entire manufacturing sector has undergone a general skill upgrading. As a result, from 1983 to 2002, "employment in high skilled manufacturing occupations has risen an impressive 37 percent" (Deitz and Orr, 2006, p. 2). This increase in high-wage jobs is most evident in the areas of "engineering, research and development, and other specialized fields" (p. 2).

Although it is difficult to assess the short-term impact of any given change in technology on employment in any particular industry, looking at the economy as a whole over the long run, we can see the benefits more clearly. As the leading textbook in labor economics states, "There is no evidence that technological change (over the course of this [twentieth] century, say) has led to permanent problems of unemployment. In fact, real wages have risen rather dramatically from their levels earlier this century, a rise that has been at least partly fueled by technological change" (Ehrenberg and Smith, 1997, p. 126). As we have argued, during the process of economic development, we also see that "technological change is more likely to increase the demand for skilled than for unskilled labor" (Ehrenberg and Smith, 1997, p. 126). This carves out a role for education in providing new workers with an opportunity to acquire the skills necessary for the emerging economy and in retraining older workers to fit these higher skill sets. Every study of future labor markets suggests that it is not the lack of jobs that we must worry about but rather the lack of skilled workers to fill the jobs created by the new manufacturing and knowledge economy.

Rising Skill Levels and Work Teams

The idea that technological change raises the skill levels required of workers is empirically documented in an important article by Autor, Levy, and Murnane (2003). They show that from 1960 to 1998, computerization in American industries "reduced the input of labor doing routine manual and routine cognitive tasks and increased labor input of non-routine cognitive tasks" (p. 1281). Using complex modeling and a vast array of historical data, they conclude that changes in workplace tasks stemming from this computerization was the underlying cause of the increased demand for college-educated labor in those industries. Similar patterns can be found in other industries as new techniques are introduced. This does not mean that all low-skill jobs will eventually be eliminated, but it does mean that most of the highest-wage jobs will require the higher-level skills associated with postsecondary education. In the case of computers, for instance, "tasks demanding flexibility, creativity, general problem solving, and complex communications—what we call non-routine cognitive tasks—do not (yet) lend themselves to computerization" (Autor, Levy, and Murnane, 2003, p. 1284). At least for the time being, these are the skills that colleges should focus on developing.

Research has also shown that as work tasks become more complex, workers in both small and large firms are increasingly grouped together in problem-solving teams. In a review of this research, Lazear and Shaw (2007) state that "from 1987 to 1996, the share of large firms that have more than 20 percent of their workers in production teams rose from 37 percent to 66 percent, while the percent with workers in self-managed work teams rose from 27 to 78 percent" (p. 4). The ability to work in teams, communicate with an increasingly diverse labor force, and think critically to solve problems are the skills and dispositions that higher education is well equipped to deliver. It is fortunate that the very general education goals that produce desirable citizenship and social good also dovetail with producing a more productive workforce. As Carnevale (2008) has suggested, "the economic value of general competencies exceeds and is growing faster than job-specific competencies" (p. 28).

Much of what we have said about technological change can be repeated with respect to increased trade and globalization. In recent years, however, the outsourcing of what previously were considered safe service jobs and the entry of China and India into the global marketplace have caused a great deal of uncertainty about whether the new jobs created by technological change and international trade will be staying in the United States.

Increased Globalization and Trade

It is generally acknowledged that the modern world has experienced two periods of rapid globalism and increased world trade. The first phase, from 1850 to 1913, was propelled by technological change that lowered the cost of transporting goods. The second era started around 1960 and continues into the present. During the second half of the twentieth century, the increase in trade was again driven by a rapid drop in transport costs, and as we moved into the twenty-first century, this was joined by the revolutions in telecommunications and the use of the Internet (Hummels, 2007). What was true for world trade was also true for the United States. In the second era of globalization, the value of U.S. exports plus imports "rose from 6.5 percent of GDP in 1960 to around 20 percent of GDP in the early 2000s" (Hummels, 2007, p. 131).

Operating in much the same way as technological change, trade increases productivity by moving resources, including labor, to the more productive sectors of the economy. We have argued that technological change has a bias that gives an advantage to high-skilled occupations. Some now wonder if globalization has a bias against high-wage countries that will drain them of these jobs through offshoring.

A popular expression of the threat of offshoring can be found in Thomas L. Friedman's best-selling book *The World Is Flat* (2005). (For a critique of this book by an orthodox economist, see Leamer, 2007.) Friedman describes how the second phase of globalism, with its advances in software capabilities, low-cost telecommunications, and transportation, is now enabling the increased movement of people, ideas, and goods and services across national borders.

How much offshoring is occurring? Most studies indicate that the volume of jobs lost to the current wave of offshoring is not very large. The popular media are full of real stories of hardship, often followed by exaggerated claims of the extent of the problem. For a more balanced view, we recommend an article in *Foreign Affairs* written by Alan S. Blinder, a professor of economics at Princeton and former vice chairman of the board of governors of Federal Reserve Bank. Although Blinder believes we "should not view the coming wave of offshoring as an impending catastrophe," he cautions us that economists may have "underestimated both the importance of offshoring and its disruptive effect on wealthy countries" (Blinder, 2006, p. 113).

The most commonly cited estimate of the extent of the offshoring of jobs from the United States, done by Forrester Research, projects that perhaps 3.3 million white-collar jobs will be moved overseas by 2015, an average of about 300,000 jobs a year. That sounds like a lot, but in an economy that has approximately 140 million jobs, it is only 0.2 percent of total employment. In fact, in the United States, close to 30 million jobs turn over every year, and the vast majority of the jobs lost are the result of changing technology and consumer taste, not globalization. That is not to say, however, that some offshoring is not occurring and is not a threat to some jobs.

The kinds of jobs that are the most susceptible to offshoring are some of the very jobs that community colleges target for their technical and vocational graduates. The jobs that are the most threatened are those that involve routine tasks that can be digitized. The media are replete with examples of manufacturing processes, accounting operations, x-ray analyses, and other job activities that have been offshored. Students responding to the media or listening to those who have lost jobs are gravitating toward jobs requiring more creativity or face-to-face contact, such as teaching, nursing, food service, and law enforcement.

The most common solution to the problem of the loss of jobs due to offshoring is to educate people to the highest level possible. However, more education might not be enough, as many high-skill jobs such as software design and product development are also vulnerable to offshoring, where they will be done by lower-wage workers. In fact, as Blinder (2006) notes, "The critical divide in the future may be between those types of work that can be easily deliverable through [a wire or wireless] connection . . . and those that cannot. This unconventional divide does not correspond well to traditional distinctions between jobs that require high levels of education and jobs that do not" (p. 118). It is difficult to predict at this point which jobs will be vulnerable to offshoring and what kinds of new jobs will be created and insourced to the United States as a result of the global economy. Community colleges will still be called on to provide training for "a few good electrical engineering technicians" or other specialties. If a new manufacturing plant moves into a region, the local community college, being sensitive to the costs and shelf life of programs developed, will respond with the necessary training.

The Role of Education

Although much of our discussion in this chapter has emphasized the job losses due to the impact of technological change and globalization, we should not lose sight of the fact that these forces, among others, will also expand the need for a more skilled workforce. Once we get by the current cyclical downturn, our larger problem is finding enough skilled workers for the future as well as strengthening the safety net that retrains those who are caught in the transition between the old economy and the emerging one.

Changing Technology. Since the direction of technological change is impossible to predict, the most that colleges can do is to react as fast as possible to changes in the market. One might reasonably guess, for instance, that two of the industries of the future will revolve around nanotechnology and biotechnology. These infant industries are currently dominated by the United States, but the jobs of the future that might fit into the community college mission have not been invented yet. Community colleges on public funding cannot afford to start expensive programs on anticipated changes in technology that may never materialize. While the long-run impact of technological change on the demand for educated labor looks quite favorable, colleges have to deal in the real world of the short run. Programs cannot be initiated without a clear and current demand for the skills these graduates will possess. However, workers in transition between older and newer processes of production can be retrained for jobs that exist now. But this can be a costly process and may not work as well with older workers (Ehrenberg and Smith, 1997, pp. 325–26). Dealing with these problems and keeping the U.S. labor market as flexible as possible will require policies on the national level to promote full employment, increased labor mobility, and the funding of more effective retraining programs for displaced workers.

Globalization. When it comes to anticipating change due to globalization we can be a little more prescriptive. Higher education, including community colleges, can provide students with more global competencies and produce graduates who have the ability to engage in multinational workforce activities at home or abroad. But although the demands of the new global environment are apparent, a recent study by the American Council on Education finds that academia has been slow in responding to these challenges through internationalization of its curricula and campuses (Green and Siaya, 2005). Dellow (2007) has recommended that occupational and technical programs monitor more aggressively how their occupational labor markets are changing globally, understand how their occupations are changing locally, and work continuously with business and industry to adapt academic programs to workplace realities. Those realities will include not only new technology but also some of the same global competencies necessary for occupations that require the bachelor's degree and higher.

NEW DIRECTIONS FOR COMMUNITY COLLEGES • DOI: 10.1002/cc

Olney (2008) recently completed a survey of 143 businesses and industries in the Tampa Bay, Florida, region to determine which, if any, global competencies employers thought community college students and graduates should possess. Foreign language and cross-cultural competencies emerged as the global competencies that businesses in the area viewed as most beneficial to their business competitiveness.

A Perennial Challenge. National statistics on completion rates and attendance patterns indicate that less than 50 percent of those who enter associate degree programs graduate or transfer to universities (Adelman, 2005). Through improved retention and transfer policies, we can probably improve somewhat on this percentage. However, for the countless tens of thousands of community college students who do not have the time, money, interest, or ability to pursue a more liberal and global education, there may be a need for programming that provides a more practical education, providing the necessary skills to get a decent job in their communities. These individuals will need to understand that they run the risk of changing jobs more frequently than professionals and will need to continually seek additional training and education to remain employed.

Conclusion

In light of the forces outlined in this chapter, here are some of the campus issues to consider:

- It seems clear that workers will require higher-level math and science skills, more creative thinking, and a greater ability to communicate and interact with workers from other cultures and countries if they are to compete in a global economy and adapt to changing technology. The ability to work in teams, as well as having greater knowledge of other countries, their cultures, and their languages, will be an asset, if not a requirement.
- In our degree programs, we should be careful not to let courses that teach specific workplace skills crowd out the broader general education courses that not only produce better citizens but also build a more flexible and transferable educational foundation. Doing this without adding to the total number of credits required for the degree will take careful planning.
- Many of the higher-skilled jobs will require a bachelor's degree or more. We should push more students in this direction. The students who transfer to baccalaureate programs will have the opportunity to further develop the necessary skills and dispositions.
- We need to take the remedial function more seriously. If not, the more than 40 percent of our student population who need remedial work will fall through the cracks and add to the nation's problem of growing income inequality. However, this is a short-term fix. In the long run, we lack the time and resources to remediate students. We need to work with high schools to improve the skills of the students we receive so that we

NEW DIRECTIONS FOR COMMUNITY COLLEGES • DOI: 10.1002/cc

can concentrate on developing the higher-level ones necessary for the new economy.

- There will be continuing conflict between the demand for short-term responsive programs and the emerging need for competencies more typical of general education. While some forces will drive us to expand our transfer function, others will require a greater use of the short-term corporate training model. Campus leadership will be challenged to find and allocate resources to these seemingly disparate and necessary educational endeavors.

- The shifting job market will require us to develop more opportunities for lifelong learning and teach students how to engage in it as self-directed learners. This is especially important for students who do not transfer to obtain advanced degrees because they will be required to change jobs more frequently in the future.

- Maintaining flexibility will require more systematic and frequent assessment of business and industry needs, and these assessments will need to include more analysis of labor market and global trends. The traditional method of curriculum development will not result in viable programs with reasonable "shelf lives" unless the process takes into account these trends.

Conclusion

The problems and issues described in this chapter require major discussion and swift action on campuses. Every community college president who speaks to local constituents is sure to emphasize how the college is there to serve local community needs. Those who think seriously about the future will realize that in order to do so in our rapidly changing economy, community college educators must once again reinvent themselves to find ways of responding to events halfway around the world or, better yet, anticipating them.

References

Adelman, C. *Moving into Town—and Moving On: The Community College in the Lives of Traditional-Age Students.* Washington, D.C.: U.S. Department of Education, 2005.

Autor, D. H., Levy, F., and Murnane, R. J. "The Skill Content of Recent Technological Change: An Exploration." *Quarterly Journal of Economics,* 2003, *118*(4), 1279–1333.

Blinder, A. S. "Offshoring: The Next Industrial Revolution." *Foreign Affairs,* 2006, *85*(2), 113–128.

Carnevale, A. P. "College for All?" *Change,* Jan.–Feb. 2008, pp. 23–29.

Deitz, R., and Orr, J. "A Leaner, More Skilled U.S. Manufacturing Workforce." *Current Issues in Economics and Finance,* 2006, *12*(2).

Dellow, D. A. "The Role of Globalization in Technical and Occupational Programs." In E. J. Valeau and R. L. Raby (eds.), *International Reform Efforts and Challenges in Community Colleges.* New Directions for Community Colleges, no. 138. San Francisco: Jossey-Bass, 2007.

Ehrenberg, R. G., and Smith, R. S. *Modern Labor Economics.* Reading, Mass.: Addison-Wesley, 1997.

Franklin, J. C. "An Overview of BLS Projections to 2016." *Monthly Labor Review*, 2007, *130*(11), 3–12.

Friedman, T. *The World Is Flat: A Brief History of the Twenty-First Century.* New York: Farrar, Straus & Giroux, 2005.

Green, M., and Siaya, L. *Measuring Internationalization at Community Colleges.* Washington, D.C.: American Council on Education, 2005.

Hummels, D. "Transportation Costs and International Trade in the Second Era of Globalization." *Journal of Economic Perspectives*, 2007, *21*(3), 131–154.

Lazear, E. P., and Shaw, K. L. "Personnel Economics: The Economist's View of Human Resources." *Journal of Economic Perspectives*, 2007, *21*(4), 91–114.

Leamer, E. E. "A Flat World, a Level Playing Field, a Small World After All, or None of the Above? A Review of Thomas Friedman's *The World Is Flat.*" *Journal of Economic Literature*, 2007, *45*(1), 83–126.

Olney, R. "U.S.-Based Business Needs for Technical/Occupational Employees with International Skills: Considerations for Community College and Sub- Baccalaureate Programs in the Tampa Bay Economic Zone." Unpublished doctoral dissertation, University of South Florida, 2008.

RICHARD M. ROMANO *is the director of the Institute for Community College Research at Broome Community College in Binghamton, New York, and a research associate at the Institute for Community Development and the Cornell Higher Education Research Institute at Cornell University.*

DONALD A. DELLOW *was president of Broome Community College in Binghamton, New York, for fifteen years and is now associate professor of higher education at the University of South Florida.*

3

This chapter argues that postsecondary competencies and awards have become the threshold requirement for middle-class earnings and status.

Help Wanted: Postsecondary Education and Training Required

Anthony P. Carnevale, Jeff Strohl, Nicole Smith

For most of the twentieth century, high school was enough for a shot at middle-class status and wages. Today no one goes anywhere in the American job market without some postsecondary education or training.

The increasing importance of education and training beyond high school in allocating economic opportunity results from broad social and economic trends.
These are the major trends: the rise of the global knowledge economy; the slow and painful demise of the American blue-collar economy in which workers, mostly white males, earned good wages with a high school education or less; welfare reform and the emergence of "work first" as the guiding principle in social policy; and a society where men, women, and youth are fully mobilized at work.

The notion that some kind of postsecondary education and training has become the threshold requirement for middle-class earnings and status has not been lost on the American public. More than two-thirds of Americans go on to postsecondary education or training after high school, although only 34 percent of students in eighth grade will later go on to get a degree from a two-year or four-year school. Access to college has become the essential goal for K–12 education. Middle-class employability is now the penultimate standard for K–16 educational adequacy (authors' calculations using data from National Center for Education Statistics, 1988, and CPS Utilities, 2007).

NEW DIRECTIONS FOR COMMUNITY COLLEGES, no. 146, Summer 2009 © 2009 Wiley Periodicals, Inc.
Published online in Wiley InterScience (www.interscience.wiley.com) • DOI: 10.1002/cc.363

Data from the Current Population Survey (CPS) show that between 1973 and 2007, the share of prime-age workers, between thirty and fifty-nine years old, with at least some college increased from 28 percent to almost 60 percent. Over that same period, the share with a B.A. or better doubled from 16 percent to 32 percent, while the share of subbaccalaureate attainment more than doubled from 12 percent to 28 percent. Associate degree holders currently comprise a third of the subbaccalaureate workforce while those with some college but no A.A. or B.A. comprise roughly two-thirds (authors' calculations from data in CPS, 2007). The rising tide in career-related human capital development has come in every venue and shows that the full array of degrees, certificates, and other awards is not captured by the traditional degree categories.

One of the more striking trends in these data is the steady increase in female participation over males below the doctoral level. Average earnings increase progressively with the standard hierarchy of certificates and degrees. The difference between male and female wage hierarchies is one possible explanation for the relative increase in female participation in postsecondary education; earning less at each degree level, women need more postsecondary education to make male wages.

More education is generally better than less, but the curriculum and the occupational focus are sometimes more important.

Until recently the economic value of education has largely been a matter of degrees: whoever had the most education and the highest degree level got the best jobs. As education connects more closely with the economy and the share of Americans going on to postsecondary education, however, these historical relationships between degree attainment and earnings are changing. Now it matters not only if you go and graduate; what you take, where you go, and what occupation or industry you enter into matter more and more. The earnings differences among people with different degree levels are growing. For instance, 22 percent of those with an occupational or vocational A.A. earn more than the median earnings of those with a B.A. and 14 percent earn more than the median earnings of people with graduate degrees. In turn, 25 percent of those with a B.A. earn less than those with an A.A. degree, and 23 percent earn less than those with a license or certificate but not an A.A. Not only is the overlap between people with different degrees growing, but so are the earnings differences among people with the same degree.

The strength of the relationship between postsecondary education and opportunity has increased in both the real economy and American politics.

Americans welcome the increasing reliance on postsecondary education as the arbiter of economic opportunity because, in theory, it allows us to expand merit-based opportunity without surrendering individual responsibility. After all, we each have to do our own homework to make the grades and do well on the tests that get us into college and in line for good jobs. Education-based opportunity complements our other key preferences for an open economy and a limited government. Education has become the nation's preferred third way between the economic instability that comes with runaway global markets and the individual dependency that Americans associate with the welfare state.

The growing economic power of postsecondary education allows us to anchor economic opportunity in individual talent and effort without government interference in the economy or the labor market.

With no substantial terminal vocational alternative in high school, "College for All" and its homely country cousin, "Postsecondary Education and Training for All," resonate with our recent experience on the ground in the real economy.

Most new jobs that require postsecondary preparation have been created in white-collar office jobs, education and health care jobs, and high-tech jobs—the signature occupations and industries in the often-cited "new knowledge economy."

The increasing reliance on postsecondary education as the arbiter of opportunity is a direct result of the rise of the postindustrial service economy and the increasing share of office workers. The share of white-collar office jobs, the workforce in the new service economy, has risen from 30 to 40 percent since 1973. In 1973, only 38 percent of office workers had some kind of postsecondary education. Today 69 percent of office workers have some postsecondary education: almost 40 percent have at least a bachelor's degree, 10 percent have associate degrees, and more than 20 percent have some college but no degree, making office work one of the most highly educated job sectors.

The health care and education sectors continue to grow as developing and maintaining human capital become more important in the knowledge economy. Since the 1970s, education and health care jobs have increased from 10 percent to almost 20 percent of all jobs. The share of education and health care jobs with at least some college increased from fewer than half in the 1970s to more than 75 percent today, with more than 52 percent with a bachelor's or graduate degree, 11 percent with an associate degree, and 12 percent with some college but no degree.

The share of technology jobs has doubled from roughly 4 to 8 percent of all jobs. In 1973, 63 percent of technology workers had at least some college, while 86 percent now have postsecondary education. More than half have at least a bachelor's degree, 16 percent have an associate degree, and almost 20 percent have some college but no degree.

Factory jobs are shrinking both proportionally and in absolute numbers. Since 1960, the factory share has fallen from 32 to 17 percent. New technology and high-performance work processes combine to enable manufacturers to produce more goods while using fewer but more highly skilled

NEW DIRECTIONS FOR COMMUNITY COLLEGES • DOI: 10.1002/cc

workers. Since 1960, the United States has increased real manufacturing output by nearly 3 percent annually without increasing the number of production workers. In 1973, only 12 percent of workers on the factory floor had any college, but that percentage has now increased to more than 36 percent. Roughly 6 percent have a bachelor's degree or better, 8 percent have an associate degree, and 17 percent have some college but no degree.

Like factory jobs, natural resource jobs, including farming, fishing, forestry, and mining, are in decline both as a share of the economy and in actual jobs. Natural resource jobs accounted for about 5 percent of all jobs in 1959. These jobs had declined by more than two-thirds and now account for only about 1.5 percent of all jobs in the economy. In 1973, two-thirds of these workers were high school dropouts; now workers with at least some college hold 31 percent of these jobs.

Low-wage service jobs are a mixed bag of transitional jobs and career jobs. The share of low-wage services jobs has not grown since the 1950s, remaining at about one-fifth, or about 28 million, of the available jobs. We tend to overestimate the importance of low-wage service jobs in the dynamic that links learning and careers. Many of the people in these jobs are young, sometimes in school, in transition to something better, or are older workers in transition to retirement. This is especially true for workers below the age of twenty-five who will likely move on to better jobs when they complete their education or training.

The increase in the wage premium for employees with postsecondary education relative to high school graduates is the most significant signal that the economy is demanding more postsecondary-level workers.

During the 1960s and 1970s, the wage premium for postsecondary education fell, but throughout the 1980s and 1990s, the wage premium for workers with postsecondary education began to climb again. CPS data show that the wage advantage for postsecondary education has generally held up and even improved in spite of a huge increase in the supply of college-educated workers.

Between 1983 and 2007, the number of prime-age workers with some college but no degree increased by 11 million people (from 6 to 17 million workers), rising from 9 percent to 17 percent of the workforce. Their average wages increased from $22,571 to $29,070 in 2007 dollars. Between 1983 and 2007 the number of prime-age workers with associate degrees increased from 7.6 to 9.1 million workers. Their real wages increased from $25,000 to $33,000. And over the same period, the number of those with a bachelor's degree increased from 10 to 20 million, and in spite of the increased supply, their average real wages increased from $33,000 to $48,000. And the number of prime-age workers with a master's degree or higher increased from 4 to 10 million. Their average real wages increased from $45,000 to $72,000.

Since the 1970s the share of workers with at least some college tripled, while their wage advantages over workers with high school educations almost doubled over the same period. This development is remarkable: usually when the supply of anything increases, its price goes down. Since the 1990s, employed workers with at least some college increased by 32 percent or 18.4 million new workers, divided equally among workers with a bachelor's degree or higher and subbaccalaureate college workers.

Postsecondary education and training have become the nation's workforce qualification and development system outside the workplace by both design and default.
Society has flirted with an alternative second-chance workplace education and training system dedicated to workforce development and retraining for economic adjustment, but all that has been learned from the second-chance system is that what counts is the first chance at K–16 education. For now, the second-chance system has been all but abandoned. Federal funding for workplace training, in real 2003 dollars, declined from $27 billion in the last Carter budget to about $3 billion in the 2007 Bush budget.

The emergence of postsecondary institutions as the primary workforce development institutions outside the labor market is evident in the gradual but relentless movement toward vocational, occupational, and professional education in postsecondary programs. For example, of the almost 1.4 million bachelor's degrees awarded in 2004, 42,106 were conferred in the liberal arts and sciences, general studies, and humanities. More than 80 percent of master's degrees and 60 percent of doctorates are awarded in nonacademic fields. The same pattern is reinforced in the expansion in applied associate degrees, certificates, certifications, and customized training. Of the 665,301 associate degrees awarded in 2004, 227,650 were conferred in the liberal arts and sciences, general studies, and humanities, and only 801 were conferred in mathematics.

If the immediate past is any guide, the future promises more of the same.
Projections that we prepared for the U.S. Senate Committee on Health, Education, Labor, and Pensions using both U.S. Census and Bureau of Labor Statistics data show that between 2002 and 2012, there will be 24 million new jobs for workers with associate, bachelor's, and graduate degrees, a 30 percent increase.

Will we be able to meet the future demand for college workers if we rely on America's own college workforce? Not easily. Baby boom retirements should create a steady stream of replacement openings for college-educated workers; by 2020, for example, there will be 40 million college-educated baby boomers between the ages of fifty-five and seventy-five. Census data show that the United States is not producing college-educated workers fast enough to replace retiring baby boomers. Between 1980 and 2000, we increased the share of workers with at least some college by a hefty 20 percent. At current rates of college enrollment, the share of workers with at least some college will increase by only 3 percent between 2000 and 2020.

To counter this projected shortage, competition for college workers could increase wages and encourage college enrollment and graduation. But rising college wages over the past thirty years have not resulted in supply catching up with demand. In the future, the increasing size of the global college workforce could hold college wages down in the United States, blunting incentive effects, as it already has in engineering and information technology. The United States could move toward a skill-based immigration strategy to import more college workers.

The United States could also delay retirement for college-educated baby boomers by squeezing access to social security and health care, but political opposition would be significant. Our estimates indicate that delaying retirements by delaying government benefits will mostly affect workers with no postsecondary education or training, who are most dependent on government retirement benefits. And although older workers are more experienced, those with postsecondary preparation and a lifetime of wage progress are also expensive relative to younger workers in America and the rest of the world.

It does seem intuitively sensible that workers will want to work longer as life expectancy rises. Baby boomers are indeed working longer, but actuaries have no evidence thus far that the change in retirement behavior will compensate for the sheer volume of retirees and the flattening of educational attainment among younger cohorts.

The wild card in the economic future role of college education as the arbiter of economic opportunity is the global economy.

In the 1970s and 1980s, low-skill, low-wage jobs went overseas, but beginning in the late 1990s, 70 percent of offshored jobs have required at least some college. With the addition of Brazil, Russia, India, and China, the size of the earth's capitalist workforce has doubled, reducing the U.S. share of the world's college-level workers from about 30 to 15 percent. And foreign college workers will be a lot cheaper than American workers for decades to come.

So far, offshoring has been a trickle: a few hundred thousand jobs a year at most. Moreover, an authoritative McKinsey study (2005) estimates that only about 3 to 5 million people in Brazil, Russia, India, and China have the appropriate postsecondary skills and English-speaking abilities necessary to substitute for American workers with postsecondary education.

Although the actual level of offshoring has been relatively low, the potential for it is much larger. Our preliminary analysis demonstrates three levels of potential offshoring risk in the current American workforce. Using our criteria, we find that there appear to be about 8 million jobs where risk is as high as 80 percent, about 22 million jobs where risk is roughly 50 percent, and as many as 40 million American jobs that are theoretically vulnerable if we include risk levels below 50 percent.

The potential for offshoring is not just about losing the postsecondary jobs in the United States; it's also about capital flows and their effect on future jobs. The balance of capital flows in and out of the United States can leverage an invisible offshoring of college jobs if America loses its magnetic pull on global capital. The ability to attract and retain financial capital and focus investments on high-value-added jobs that generally require at least some college is just as important as keeping existing college jobs.

While the risks of offshoring can be scary, static analysis of offshoring risk tends to overstate the risks and understate the opportunities, especially in the United States, the world's most dynamic labor market.
The United States creates and destroys jobs faster than any other economy in the world. Moreover, the central tendency in this process of creative destruction is to increase skill and earnings levels. According to Vollman's analysis of wage record data (personal communication, July 2008), every three months, nearly 14 million workers will be hired and 13.6 million will leave their current jobs. More than half of those actions will happen because a new job was created or a job disappeared. The rest will be because someone was moving between jobs or on or off unemployment. We offer three additional observations to demonstrate the dynamism of the American economy:

- Every year, more than a third of the entire U.S. labor force changes jobs.
- Every year, more than 30 million Americans are working in jobs that did not exist in the previous quarter.
- Many of the occupations workers have today did not exist five years ago.

We need to keep this constant churning in mind while considering the likely impact of offshoring and other disruptive forces in American labor markets.

If we want to increase the number of students who enroll and graduate from postsecondary institutions, the "low-hanging fruit" are the more than half a million college-qualified students from working families who are lost along the way in high school.
There are more than half a million students, mostly from working class and low-income families, who complete high school in the top half of their classes but never earn an associate, bachelor's, or a graduate degree within eight years of high school graduation. Among these college-qualified students who do not attend college or do not graduate within eight years of high school graduation:

Twenty-three percent, or 129,000 of the 559,000 top students, come from families in the top income quartile ($83,001 and above in 2005, with a median of $145,000).

Thirty-three percent, or 185,000 of the 559,000 top students, come from families in the second income quartile from the top ($50,280 to $83,000 in 2005, with a median of $65,512).

Twenty-five percent, or 140,000 of the 559,000 top students, come from families in the third income quartile from the top ($26,730 to $50,279 in 2005, with a median of $38,306).

Nineteen percent, or 106,000 of the 559,000 top students, come from families in the bottom income quartile ($26,729 or less in 2005, with a median of $15,000).

As many as 11 million adults and out-of-school youth could benefit from postsecondary education and training, especially in community colleges, but they are unlikely to be served.

According to an analysis of the National Adult Literacy Survey (National Center for Education Statistics, 1992), roughly half of low-income workers and out-of-school youth have literacy levels that qualify them for college-level work. The share of qualified prisoners is roughly 30 percent, and the share of dislocated workers qualified for postsecondary education or training could be as high as 60 percent (Kirsch and Jungeblut, 1992; Kirsch, Jungeblut, Jenkins, and Kolstad, 1993). If trained, they could add more than $120 billion to the national wealth. And in the case of prisoners, recidivism could be reduced by as much as 29 percent (Steurer, Smith, and Tracy, 2001).

While the benefits of providing postsecondary education and training are powerful and growing, so are the barriers to access, especially for nontraditional students.

The funding barriers are the most daunting, especially for community colleges whose missions keep expanding and whose revenue base keeps contracting relative to other public and private providers.

Part of the community college funding problem results from the fact that the postsecondary funding system is not nearly as flexible as the community colleges themselves. Initially founded as junior colleges, these schools became community-based teaching institutions and took on an increasingly occupational role in local labor markets for place-bound students of all ages. The community college gradually outgrew its marginalized status as a "junior" to four-year institutions. Its emergence as an alternative to the traditional four-year college came with an implicit rebuke to the class- and race-based meritocratic elitism of the selective four-year institutions and established an emphasis on open admissions, community service, and upward mobility in the postsecondary system.

With the knowledge economy firmly in the saddle by the 1980s, the community college began expanding its mission at both ends of the curriculum in response to market demands. Community colleges became major players in course and course-cluster-based shadow education and training system. The shadow system of nondegreed courses offers three kinds of value: courses and clusters of courses that provide basic skills which allow further learning on the job and in formal courses, provide transferable credits for further education, and provide immediate earnings returns and career mobility in labor markets.

In addition to the expansion of courses and course clusters with bite-sized value, community colleges have expanded formal award and degree offerings. These colleges have reacted to the constant upward ratcheting in degree requirements in every occupation that results from the upskilling dynamic ultimately tied to globalization. As degree requirements increase, community colleges have begun offering bachelor's degrees and postgraduate certificates, especially in occupations and professions with strong ties to local labor markets such as education, health care, and information technology.

As the community college adapts to meet core mission goals of market responsiveness and upward mobility, its attachment to localism and open admissions comes into conflict. The simultaneous growth of the noncredit shadow curriculum, the postsecondary system, and the bachelor's degree is dawning as "the age of and" in community colleges: they must strive to be loyal to democratic *and* meritocratic values, to be both global *and* locally responsive, to be internally coherent *and* externally responsive, to be providers of occupational liberal arts *and* professional curricula, and to be governed by community-based university *and* corporate systems. The result is an increasingly complex identity, an effect typical of globally responsive institutions. Thus, while community colleges have adapted to new realities, financing systems have not. State funding has declined as a share of community college revenue.

Federal funding is still overwhelmingly based on individual student aid, making no adjustments for the varied cost structures of the community college missions. Overall decline in the relative value of public aid and one-size-fits-all cost structures dilutes the community colleges' ability to fund every mission, especially nondegreed learning targeted to the neediest students.

Absent new public money, the funding squeeze, especially in public community colleges, will only get worse because the current funding crisis in postsecondary education reflects structural as well as cyclical changes in public postsecondary funding. As the share of state budgets going to higher education has fallen off by 13 percent since 1990, the share going to Medicaid has increased by two-thirds and the share going to prisons has increased by one-third. And since the last recession in 2000, state budgets have gone from bad to worse, forcing dramatic tuition increases in public institutions. The 2008 recession has triggered a new downward spiral in public funding at the state level. The federal higher education budget is undergoing a similar squeeze as tax cuts combine with a shift in resources toward health care, social security, and national defense.

As money gets tighter, the traditional upper-middle-class eighteen- to twenty-four-year-old student becomes the preferred client in postsecondary education. These students arrive with tuition in hand, are assembled on campus, sit in large classes scheduled during normal working hours, and are taught standardized academic curricula.

In these tough budgetary times, the least attractive student clients are the nontraditional students, especially those with work and family responsibilities.

Low-income adults and out-of-school youth need more financial aid than the traditional eighteen- to twenty-four-year-old student, and adult students are more expensive because they need to integrate their studies seamlessly with work and family needs. They require more expensive courses that mix applied and academic learning, flexible scheduling that increases personnel and facilities costs, and family services such as child care and counseling to hold it all together and plan for future transitions. The footloose and fancy-free traditional student can afford mistakes that adults with jobs and families cannot. Low-income adults also may require remedial or refresher courses that no one wants to pay for, along with customized work-oriented courses that often need to be offered in bite-sized, nondegreed chunks which are not eligible for federal subsidies and are funded, and then only partly, by a minority of states.

The accountability movement continues to be bad news for nontraditional students who tend to concentrate in community colleges.

What makes matters even worse is that the increasing cost of higher education has inspired an accountability movement that may be good news for traditional students but continues to be bad news for nontraditional students. Accountability measures tend to focus on increasing degree attainment, reducing time to graduation, reducing dropouts and loan defaults, and funding only nonremedial degreed courses and higher standards for student learning outcomes. The problem for low-income adults is that the combined effect of reduced financial support and higher standards encourages colleges to cater to the most well-heeled and well-prepared young students who are least likely to be distracted by work and family.

The worst-case scenario that confronts us is that the financial strains emerging in higher education will result in a gradual and silent abandonment of working families and nontraditional students.

In an economy where good jobs require postsecondary education and training, the growing economic divide between those with and those without postsecondary education and training will continue to widen, fostering intergenerational reproduction of economic and cultural elites inimical to our democratic ethos and our worthiness for leadership in the global contest of cultures.

NEW DIRECTIONS FOR COMMUNITY COLLEGES • DOI: 10.1002/cc

References

CPS Utilities. *Current Population Survey, 1973–2007*. Los Angeles: Unicon Research Corporation, Mar. 2007.

Kirsch, I. S., and Jungeblut, A. *Profiling the Literacy Proficiencies of JTPA and ES/UI Populations*. Princeton, N.J.: Educational Testing Service, 1992.

Kirsch, I. S., Jungeblut, A., Jenkins, L., and Kolstad, A. *Adult Literacy in America*. Washington, D.C.: U.S. Government Printing Office, 1993.

McKinsey and Company. *The Emerging Global Market*. Boston: McKinsey Global Institute, June 2005.

National Center for Education Statistics. *National Education Longitudinal Study of 1988: Base-Year to Fourth Follow-up Data Files*. Washington, D.C.: U.S. Department of Education, 1988.

National Center for Education Statistics. *National Adult Literacy Survey*. Washington, D.C.: U.S. Department of Education, 1992.

Steurer, S. J., Smith, L., and Tracy, A. *Education Reduces Crime: Three-State Recidivism Study*. Lanham, Md.: Correctional Education Association, 2001.

ANTHONY P. CARNEVALE *is president and research professor at the Georgetown University Center on Education and the Workforce.*

JEFF STROHL *is a labor economist and is director of research at the Georgetown University Center on Education and the Workforce.*

NICOLE SMITH *is a research professor at the Georgetown University Center on Education and the Workforce.*

4

This chapter contains labor market projections from the U.S. Bureau of Labor Statistics. The data set out here are used as a basis for more specific projections in the next four chapters.

National Labor Market Projections for Community College Students

Dixie Sommers

This chapter examines the job outlook for occupations where the most important path to entry is through programs typically found at the community college: an associate degree or postsecondary training but less than a degree. The chapters that follow provide a more detailed examination of particular occupational clusters.

The discussion draws on labor market projections from the U.S. Bureau of Labor Statistics (BLS), the federal agency charged with projecting long-term future labor market demand for the U.S. economy. Every two years, BLS issues ten-year projections of occupational employment and openings. Projected openings include new jobs created by economic growth and the changing structure of the economy, and openings to replace existing workers who leave their occupations for a variety of reasons, including retirement.

A Statistical Snapshot

According to the latest projections, employment between 2006 and 2016 in occupations that generally require an associate degree will grow by 18.7 percent and those requiring postsecondary vocational training will grow by 13.6 percent. These growth rates compare favorably to the 15.3 percent for occupations requiring a bachelor's degree or higher and 8.2 percent for those

---

Any conclusions presented in this chapter do not represent the position of the Bureau of Labor Statistics.

NEW DIRECTIONS FOR COMMUNITY COLLEGES, no. 146, Summer 2009 © 2009 Wiley Periodicals, Inc.
Published online in Wiley InterScience (www.interscience.wiley.com) • DOI: 10.1002/cc.364

requiring related work experience or on-the-job training (Dohm and Shniper, 2007).

It is clear from BLS data that community colleges have contributed to the increasing educational attainment of the U.S. labor force. In 2007, workers whose highest educational attainment was an associate degree accounted for 9.9 percent of the labor force age twenty-five and older, up from 7.4 percent in 1992. At the same time, the share of the labor force holding a bachelor's degree or more rose to 33.7 percent, up from 26.4 percent. The labor force share for workers with high school diplomas or less education declined from 48.1 percent in 1992 to 38.9 percent in 2007 (U.S. Bureau of Labor Statistics, Current Population Survey, 2008).

Workers age twenty-five and older with an associate degree as their highest education level also fared relatively well in the job market. Their unemployment rate was 3.0 percent in 2007, compared to 4.4 percent for high school graduates with no college and 3.6 percent for all workers age twenty-five and older. Their median weekly earnings were $740, well above the $604 for high school graduates with no college (U.S. Bureau of Labor Statistics, Current Population Survey, 2008).

Identifying Community College Occupations

An examination of the labor market prospects for community college students must look beyond associate degree holders. Community colleges deliver a variety of programs, some leading to the associate degree, some leading to nondegree credentials, and still others providing training in academic and occupational skills but no specific credential. They also prepare students for transfer to four-year institutions and completion of the bachelor's degree or higher. This variety of programs is difficult to capture in national labor market statistics.

To understand education and training requirements for entry into future jobs, BLS has developed two approaches: educational attainment clusters and education and training categories. Each approach categorizes occupations and is used to depict the requirements of projected job opportunities in those occupations.

Educational attainment clusters categorize occupations according to the educational attainment of those twenty-five to forty-four year olds working in the occupation, an age range that reflects relatively recent hiring practices for the occupation by excluding older workers. Educational attainment data show that some occupations do not belong exclusively to a particular degree or level of training. For instance, among workers twenty-five to forty-four years old employed as computer support specialists in 2006, 13 percent had a high school education or less, 44 percent had some college, and 43 percent had a college degree (U.S. Bureau of Labor Statistics, 2008). Thus, individuals with community college training may qualify for occupations where large portions of the workers hold a bachelor's degree or, alternatively, for occupations where most jobs are held by those with no college experience. However, because the educational attainment approach does not separate the associate degree holders from those with some college, the alternative education and training approach is more appropriate for our purposes.

BLS identifies eleven education and training categories that describe the most significant education and training pathway to employment for each occupation. The categories range from professional and doctoral degrees to occupations requiring only moderate to short-term training but no degree.

Each of the 753 occupations for which BLS produces projections is assigned to one, and only one, of the education and training categories. BLS describes the method as an analytical process: "BLS economists assign one of these categories to each occupation based on their judgment and knowledge, acquired through analysis of data from BLS itself and from other government and private organizations, and through interviews with many sources including representatives of professional and trade associations, unions, and employers; educators; and training experts" (U.S. Bureau of Labor Statistics, 2008).

The education and training categories provide a straightforward method of describing occupations that take into account experience and on-the-job training. For occupations with a variety of entry paths, however, the categories cannot capture this variety because each occupation is assigned to only one category.

To examine the community college labor market, we make use of two education and training categories, associate degree and postsecondary vocational award, which we will refer to collectively as "community college occupations." Clearly the associate degree is community college training, but postsecondary awards are often provided by community colleges as well. In academic year 2005–2006, two-year institutions granted 450,800 certificates along with 584,000 associate degrees (National Center for Education Statistics, 2008). For simplicity of presentation, we collapse the remaining education and training categories into "bachelor's plus worker experience or higher degree" (the highest four categories), "bachelor's degree," and "work experience or on-the-job training" (the lowest four categories). Results are presented in Table 4.1.

The Community College Labor Market

As seen in Table 4.1, community college occupations accounted for 9.1 percent of all jobs in 2006 and are expected to generate 13.8 percent of new jobs between 2006 and 2016. These occupations are, as a group, projected to grow faster than the overall rate during this period, increasing by 15.8 percent compared to 10.4 percent for all occupations and 15.3 percent for occupations requiring a bachelor's degree or higher. Within the community

Table 4.1. Employment and Projected Job Openings by Most Significant Source of Education and Training (Employment in Thousands)

Education and Training Category	2006 Employment		2016 Employment		2006–2016 Change			2006–16 Total Job Openings Due to Growth and Net Replacement Needs	
	Total Employment	Percent Distribution	Total Employment	Percent Distribution	Numeric Change	Percent Change	Percent Distribution	Number	Percent Distribution
Total, all occupations	150,620.2	100.0%	166,220.3	100.0%	15,600.1	10.4%	100.0%	50,731.9	100.0%
Bachelor's degree or higher, including bachelor's degree plus work experience	31,270.8	20.8%	36,059.8	21.7%	4,789.1	15.3%	30.7%	10,963.9	21.6%
Community college occupations	13,712.8	9.1%	15,872.1	9.6%	2,159.9	15.8%	13.8%	4,731.3	9.3%
Associate degree	5,811.5	3.9%	6,898.7	4.2%	1,087.1	18.7%	7.0%	2,240.3	4.4%
Postsecondary vocational award	7,901.3	5.2%	8,973.4	5.4%	1,072.8	13.6%	6.9%	2,491.0	4.9%
Work experience in a related occupation, or on-the-job training	105,636.5	70.1%	114,288.3	68.8%	8,651.8	8.2%	55.5%	35,037.1	69.1%

Source: Adapted from Bureau of Labor Statistics, Monthly Labor Review, November 2007, Table 5, p. 103.

college occupations, the projected growth rate is faster: 18.7 percent for occupations where an associate degree is the most important qualification and 13.6 percent for occupations where a postsecondary vocational award is most important.

When we group all of the community college occupations into the broad categories, shown in the chapter appendix, we find that the largest concentration of jobs is in the Healthcare Practitioners and Technical occupation group, with eighteen community college occupations and 4.7 million jobs in 2006. Other groups with large job numbers are Installation, Maintenance, and Repair with fifteen occupations and nearly 1.9 million jobs, Healthcare Support with five occupations and 1.7 million jobs, and Personal Care and Service with nine occupations and 1.1 million jobs.

The appendix lists the detailed occupations assigned to the community college education and training categories. In total, ninety-one occupations are listed: forty-one from the associate degree category and fifty from the postsecondary vocational award category. The occupations range in size from 2.51 million jobs in 2006 for registered nurses to two thousand jobs for makeup artists.

The projections may be viewed in two ways: by the projected rate of job growth and the number of job openings expected. Many job openings can occur in occupations where employment is not expected to grow or even where employment decline is projected, since employers will need to replace some existing workers.

Eleven community college occupations are expected to grow by 25 percent or more, with the fastest job growth, 41.0 percent, projected for veterinary technologists and technicians. In all, fifty-four of the ninety-one community college occupations are expected to grow by more than the 10.4 percent projected for all occupations. Four community college occupations are expected to have no change in employment, and seven occupations are expected to decline. The fastest rates of decline are projected for semiconductor processors, 12.9 percent of jobs, and prepress technicians and workers, 21.1 percent.

Projected job openings include both new jobs from economic expansion as well as replacement needs. Community college occupations accounted for 9.3 percent of projected job openings for all occupations, near their 9.1 percent share of total employment in 2006 (Table 4.1). The largest number of job openings is expected in occupations that already dominate the employment count: registered nurses with 1 million openings, followed by nursing aides, orderlies, and attendants with 394,000 openings; licensed practical and licensed vocational nurses with 309,000 openings; and automotive service technicians and mechanics with 265,000 openings (see the appendix). These occupations together account for four out of ten openings in the community college occupations.

As noted earlier, workers with associate degrees had higher earnings than those with less education. A look at wages in community college occupations confirms this pattern. Annual wages in these occupations averaged $43,287 in May 2007, with occupations where associate degrees are required averaging $54,125, much higher than the $34,081 for occupations in the postsecondary award category. But we also find that associate degree occupations had lower earnings than bachelor's degree occupations ($62,083) and occupations requiring a bachelor's degree plus work experience or a degree beyond the bachelor's ($90,934) (U.S. Bureau of Labor Statistics, 2007).

Skills in Community College Occupations

The Occupational Information Network (O*NET), produced by the U.S. Department of Labor's Employment and Training Administration, provides a comprehensive database of occupational characteristics, including information on skills. O*NET provides measures for thirty-five skills, grouped into basic skills (content and process skills) and cross-functional skills (social, complex problem solving, technical, systems, and resource management skills). Each occupation is rated on each skill's importance to performance on the job (Employment and Training Administration, 2007). (For those interested in what these skills cover and for free use of the database, see http://www.onetcenter.org/content.html.)

We can use the O*NET ratings to compare the skills needed for community college occupations with those of other education and training categories. When we do, we find that the community college occupations are mostly situated between the skills necessary for jobs held by those with higher levels of education and those held by workers with lower levels of education. That is, community college occupations require lower-level content skills (such as reading comprehension, writing, mathematics, and science) than jobs held by those with a bachelor's degree. In turn, community college occupations require higher levels of these same skills than those occupations held by workers with no degree. There are a few exceptions to this in the technical skills area, but in general, community college occupations require a wide range of skills that are in a smooth continuum from lower to higher levels of education.

How BLS Does Projections

The BLS employment projections used in this volume are based on a complex method that carries with it a number of assumptions and risks.

Overview of Methods. Franklin (2007) describes the BLS projections process as "a series of analytical processes that incorporate a variety of methods, ranging from econometric and time-series models to explicitly subjective analyses" (p. 3). The process follows an orderly sequence, however, beginning with projecting the labor force and the overall economy and ending with occupational employment and replacement needs projections. In between, the industrial composition of output and employment is projected.

Labor force projections provide information on the likely future supply of workers, providing a constraint on economic growth. The general approach is to project labor force participation rates for various age, gender, race, and ethnicity groups based on examination and extrapolation of past trends. BLS then applies these rates to projections of the population in each group from the U.S. Census Bureau (Toossi, 2007).

The overall economy, including gross domestic product (GDP) and its components, is projected using a macroeconomic model supplied with the projected labor force, historical trend data, and several assumptions. These assumptions include variables such as the unemployment rate in the target year and rates of inflation and labor productivity growth over the projection period, with the labor productivity variable representing the impact of technological change. The specific assumptions for the projections from 2006 to 2016 are provided by Su (2007). The GDP projection is then translated into output by industry, resulting in commodity purchase information that is translated using a projected input-output table into industry and commodity output required to support the projected GDP.

Industry output is translated into projected wage and salary employment using information on labor hours, wages, labor productivity trends, and other factors. Self-employment for each industry is also estimated based on historical relationships between self-employment and wage and salary employment (Woods and Figueroa, 2007).

Finally, industry employment is translated into occupational employment. For each industry, 2006 information on the distribution of employment by occupation is arranged as an industry-occupation employment matrix. This matrix depicts, for example, the percentage of employment in service industries that consists of workers in information technology occupations.

These percentages, or ratios, are reviewed and, where the available information and analyst judgment warrants, adjusted to a new ratio for 2016. To the extent feasible, the impact of offshore outsourcing is incorporated into the ratio adjustments. All of these adjustments taken together, along with 2006 ratios where no adjustment is made, constitute the 2016 industry-occupation employment matrix. Extending our earlier example, the 2016 matrix shows that BLS expects network systems and data communications analysts to rise from 3.56 to 3.83 percent of employment in the computer systems design and related services industry between 2006 and 2016.

Projected occupational employment is derived by multiplying the 2016 matrix against the 2016 industry projected industry employment and summing the result by occupation. Again following our example, employment in the computer systems and related services industry is expected to rise to

1.768 million jobs. Multiplying this by the expected 3.83 percent share of the industry jobs held by network systems and data communications analysts yields a projection of the occupation's employment in the industry. Repeating this computation for every industry and summing the result for each occupation yields a total employment projection for the occupations. Finally, comparing the 2016 occupational employment to the 2006 level provides a projection of job growth or, in some occupations, decline (Dohm and Shniper, 2007).

Job growth is only one source of job opportunities, however. More, often many more, openings occur because some workers in the occupation will leave over the projection period; they may retire, leave the labor force for other reasons, or move to a job in a different occupation and will need to be replaced. BLS has developed replacement rates based on analysis of employment change in specific age-occupation cohorts (U.S. Bureau of Labor Statistics, 2008).

Risks to the Projections. The projection procedures are complex, involving many different methods, data sources, and points of analyst judgment. And they are about the future, inherently unknown. Where are they likely to go wrong?

The sources of risk to the projections are inaccuracy of the models used, assumptions that prove to be off the mark, and faulty analyst judgment. The myriad models and equations used in the projections process are based on historical relationships. While analysts examine these relationships to evaluate the results provided by the models, relationships can change in the future in ways that are not anticipated or at a faster or slower rate than the models suggest. Also, historical relationships are based on data, which may be quite accurate or may have measurement errors or other problems.

Franklin (2007) has identified some more specific risks to the 2006–2016 projections. These include the potential for significant policy change based on the aging of the U.S. population (the projections assume no major changes from current policy), higher immigration rates than those reflected in the Census Bureau's population projections, changes in the political or economic situation resulting from globalization, and the cost of energy.

Conclusion

This chapter has provided background on trends in occupations for which community college training is the most important pathway of entry. Individuals with an associate degree or other training gained in a community college may, of course, also be qualified for additional occupations where another path of entry is identified by BLS as the most important.

The next four chapters contain details on the clusters of occupations for their particular area.

NEW DIRECTIONS FOR COMMUNITY COLLEGES • DOI: 10.1002/cc

Appendix: Employment and Projected Job Openings for Community College Occupations

Occupation Title	Broad Occupation Group	Education and Training Level	Wage Rank	Employment		Employment Change			Net Replacement Needs	Growth Plus Net Replacement Needs
				2006	2016	Numeric Change	Percentage Change			
Aerospace engineering and operations technicians	Architecture and Engineering	Associate degree	VH	9	9	1	10.4		2	3
Agricultural and food science technicians	Life, Physical, and Social Science	Associate degree	H	26	28	2	6.6		4	6
Aircraft mechanics and service technicians	Installation, Maintenance, and Repair	Postsecondary vocational award	VH	122	135	13	10.6		12	25
Architectural and civil drafters	Architecture and Engineering	Postsecondary vocational award	H	116	123	7	6.1		33	40
Automotive service technicians and mechanics	Installation, Maintenance, and Repair	Postsecondary vocational award	H	773	883	110	14.3		155	265
Avionics technicians	Installation, Maintenance, and Repair	Postsecondary vocational award	VH	16	17	1	8.1		2	3
Barbers	Personal Care and Service	Postsecondary vocational award	L	60	61	1	1.1		11	12
Broadcast technicians	Arts, Design, Entertainment, Sports, and Media	Associate degree	H	38	42	5	12.1		12	17

(continues on next page)

Appendix: Employment and Projected Job Openings for Community College Occupations (continued)

Occupation Title	Broad Occupation Group	Education and Training Level	Wage Rank	Employment		Employment Change			Net Replacement Needs	Growth Plus Net Replacement Needs
				2006	2016	Numeric Change	Percentage Change			
Bus and truck mechanics and diesel engine specialists	Installation, Maintenance, and Repair	Postsecondary vocational award	H	275	306	32	11.5		60	92
Camera operators, television, video, and motion picture	Arts, Design, Entertainment, Sports, and Media	Postsecondary vocational award	H	27	30	3	11.5		5	8
Cardiovascular technologists and technicians	Healthcare Practitioners and Technical	Associate degree	H	45	57	12	25.5		6	18
Chemical technicians	Life, Physical, and Social Science	Associate degree	H	61	65	4	5.8		20	24
Civil engineering technicians	Architecture and Engineering	Associate degree	H	91	100	9	10.2		18	27
Commercial divers	Installation, Maintenance, and Repair	Postsecondary vocational award	H	3	4	1	17.7		—	1
Commercial pilots	Transportation and Material Moving	Postsecondary vocational award	VH	28	31	4	13.2		8	12
Computer specialists, all other	Computer and Mathematical Science	Associate degree	VH	136	157	21	15.1		36	57

Computer support specialists	Computer and Mathematical Science	Associate degree	H	552	624	71	12.9	171	242
Computer, automated teller, and office machine repairers	Installation, Maintenance, and Repair	Postsecondary vocational award	H	175	180	5	3.0	20	25
Court reporters	Legal	Postsecondary vocational award	H	19	24	5	24.5	3	8
Dental hygienists	Healthcare Practitioners and Technical	Associate degree	VH	167	217	50	30.1	32	82
Desktop publishers	Office and Administrative Support	Postsecondary vocational award	H	32	32	—	1.0	6	6
Diagnostic medical sonographers	Healthcare Practitioners and Technical	Associate degree	VH	46	54	9	19.1	6	15
Dietetic technicians	Healthcare Practitioners and Technical	Postsecondary vocational award	L	25	29	4	14.8	8	12
Drafters, all other	Architecture and Engineering	Postsecondary vocational award	H	25	27	3	11.0	7	10
Electric motor, power tool, and related repairers	Installation, Maintenance, and Repair	Postsecondary vocational award	H	25	24	(1)	-4.2	10	9

(continues on next page)

Appendix: Employment and Projected Job Openings for Community College Occupations (continued)

Occupation Title	Broad Occupation Group	Education and Training Level	Wage Rank	Employment		Employment Change		Net Replacement Needs	Growth Plus Net Replacement Needs
				2006	2016	Numeric Change	Percentage Change		
Electrical and electronic engineering technicians	Architecture and Engineering	Associate degree	VH	170	177	6	3.6	33	39
Electrical and electronics drafters	Architecture and Engineering	Postsecondary vocational award	VH	35	36	1	4.1	10	11
Electrical and electronics installers and repairers, transportation equipment	Installation, Maintenance, and Repair	Postsecondary vocational award	H	21	22	1	4.3	5	6
Electrical and electronics repairers, commercial and industrial equipment	Installation, Maintenance, and Repair	Postsecondary vocational award	H	80	86	5	6.8	27	32
Electrical and electronics repairers, powerhouse, substation, and relay	Installation, Maintenance, and Repair	Postsecondary vocational award	VH	22	21	(1)	-4.7	8	7
Electro-mechanical technicians	Architecture and Engineering	Associate degree	H	16	16	—	2.6	3	3
Electronic equipment installers and repairers, motor vehicles	Installation, Maintenance, and Repair	Postsecondary vocational award	L	20	21	1	4.6	6	7

Occupation	Career cluster	Education	Code						
Electronic home entertainment equipment installers and repairers	Installation, Maintenance, and Repair	Postsecondary vocational award	L	40	41	1	3.0	4	5
Embalmers	Personal Care and Service	Postsecondary vocational award	H	9	10	1	14.3	2	3
Emergency medical technicians and paramedics	Healthcare Practitioners and Technical	Postsecondary vocational award	L	201	240	39	19.2	23	62
Engineering technicians, except drafters, all other	Architecture and Engineering	Associate degree	VH	82	83	2	2.0	16	18
Environmental engineering technicians	Architecture and Engineering	Associate degree	H	21	26	5	24.8	4	9
Environmental science and protection technicians, including health	Life, Physical, and Social Science	Associate degree	H	36	47	10	28.0	14	24
Fashion designers	Arts, Design, Entertainment, Sports, and Media	Associate degree	VH	20	21	1	5.0	5	6
Fish and game wardens	Protective Service	Associate degree	H	8	8	—	-0.2	2	2
Fitness trainers and aerobics instructors	Personal Care and Service	Postsecondary vocational award	L	235	298	63	26.8	44	107
Forest and conservation technicians	Life, Physical, and Social Science	Associate degree	H	34	33	(1)	-2.0	13	12

(continues on next page)

Appendix: Employment and Projected Job Openings for Community College Occupations (continued)

Occupation Title	Broad Occupation Group	Education and Training Level	Wage Rank	Employment		Employment Change		Net Replacement Needs	Growth Plus Net Replacement Needs
				2006	2016	Numeric Change	Percentage Change		
Funeral directors	Management	Associate degree	VH	29	32	4	12.5	7	11
Gaming dealers	Personal Care and Service	Postsecondary vocational award	VL	84	104	20	24.1	17	37
Geological and petroleum technicians	Life, Physical, and Social Science	Associate degree	H	12	13	1	8.6	4	5
Hairdressers, hairstylists, and cosmetologists	Personal Care and Service	Postsecondary vocational award	L	617	694	77	12.4	74	151
Healthcare technologists and technicians, all other	Healthcare Practitioners and Technical	Postsecondary vocational award	H	79	91	12	15.0	6	18
Industrial engineering technicians	Architecture and Engineering	Associate degree	VH	75	82	7	9.9	15	22
Insurance appraisers, auto damage	Business and Financial Operations	Postsecondary vocational award	VH	13	15	2	12.5	3	5
Interior designers	Arts, Design, Entertainment, Sports, and Media	Associate degree	H	72	86	14	19.5	19	33

Occupation	Category	Education						
Jewelers and precious stone and metal workers	Production	Postsecondary vocational award	L	52	51	(1)	-2.2	9	8
Legal secretaries	Office and Administrative Support	Associate degree	H	275	308	32	11.7	44	76
Library technicians	Education, Training, and Library	Postsecondary vocational award	L	121	132	10	8.5	59	69
Licensed practical and licensed vocational nurses	Healthcare Practitioners and Technical	Postsecondary vocational award	H	749	854	105	14.0	204	309
Life, physical, and social science technicians, all other	Life, Physical, and Social Science	Associate degree	H	66	73	7	9.8	25	32
Makeup artists, theatrical and performance	Personal Care and Service	Postsecondary vocational award	H	2	3	1	39.8	—	1
Manicurists and pedicurists	Personal Care and Service	Postsecondary vocational award	VL	78	100	22	27.6	8	30
Massage therapists	Healthcare Support	Postsecondary vocational award	H	118	142	24	20.3	13	37
Mechanical drafters	Architecture and Engineering	Postsecondary vocational award	H	78	82	4	5.2	22	26

(continues on next page)

Appendix: Employment and Projected Job Openings for Community College Occupations (continued)

Occupation Title	Broad Occupation Group	Education and Training Level	Wage Rank	Employment		Employment Change		Net Replacement Needs	Growth Plus Net Replacement Needs
				2006	2016	Numeric Change	Percentage Change		
Mechanical engineering technicians	Architecture and Engineering	Associate degree	H	48	51	3	6.4	9	12
Medical and clinical laboratory technicians	Healthcare Practitioners and Technical	Associate degree	H	151	174	23	15.0	23	46
Medical equipment repairers	Installation, Maintenance, and Repair	Associate degree	H	38	46	8	21.7	11	19
Medical records and health information technicians	Healthcare Practitioners and Technical	Associate degree	L	170	200	30	17.8	46	76
Medical transcriptionists	Healthcare Support	Postsecondary vocational award	L	98	112	13	13.5	12	25
Nuclear medicine technologists	Healthcare Practitioners and Technical	Associate degree	VH	20	23	3	14.8	3	6
Nuclear technicians	Life, Physical, and Social Science	Associate degree	VH	7	7	—	6.7	2	2
Nursing aides, orderlies, and attendants	Healthcare Support	Postsecondary vocational award	L	1,447	1,711	264	18.2	130	394

Occupation	Category	Education							
Occupational therapist assistants	Healthcare Support	Associate degree	H	25	31	6	25.4	4	10
Paralegals and legal	Legal Assistants	Associate degree	H	238	291	53	22.2	31	84
Physical therapist assistants	Healthcare Support	Associate degree	H	60	80	20	32.4	8	28
Prepress technicians and workers	Production	Postsecondary vocational award	H	71	56	(15)	−21.1	11	(4)
Preschool teachers, except special education	Education, Training, and Library	Postsecondary vocational award	L	437	552	115	26.3	72	187
Psychiatric technicians	Healthcare Practitioners and Technical	Postsecondary vocational award	L	62	60	(2)	−3.3	19	17
Radiation therapists	Healthcare Practitioners and Technical	Associate degree	VH	15	18	4	24.8	2	6
Radiologic technologists and technicians	Healthcare Practitioners and Technical	Associate degree	VH	196	226	30	15.1	27	57
Real estate sales agents	Sales and Related	Postsecondary vocational award	H	432	478	46	10.6	69	115
Registered nurses	Healthcare Practitioners and Technical	Associate degree	VH	2,505	3,092	587	23.5	413	1,000

(continues on next page)

Appendix: Employment and Projected Job Openings for Community College Occupations (continued)

Occupation Title	Broad Occupation Group	Education and Training Level	Wage Rank	Employment		Employment Change		Net Replacement Needs	Growth Plus Net Replacement Needs
				2006	2016	Numeric Change	Percentage Change		
Respiratory therapists	Healthcare Practitioners and Technical	Associate degree	VH	102	126	23	22.6	15	38
Respiratory therapy technicians	Healthcare Practitioners and Technical	Associate degree	H	19	19	—	0.9	6	6
Security and fire alarm systems installers	Installation, Maintenance, and Repair	Postsecondary vocational award	H	57	68	11	20.2	8	19
Semiconductor processors	Production	Associate degree	H	42	37	(5)	–12.9	7	2
Skin care specialists	Personal Care and Service	Postsecondary vocational award	L	38	51	13	34.3	4	17
Slot key persons	Personal Care and Service	Postsecondary vocational award	L	20	22	2	11.1	4	6
Social science research assistants	Life, Physical, and Social Science	Associate degree	H	18	20	2	12.4	7	9
Sound engineering technicians	Arts, Design, Entertainment, Sports, and Media	Postsecondary vocational award	H	16	18	1	9.1	5	6

Surgical technologists	Healthcare Practitioners and Technical	Postsecondary vocational award	H	86	107	21	24.5	26	47
Telecommunications equipment installers and repairers, except line installers	Installation, Maintenance, and Repair	Postsecondary vocational award	VH	198	203	5	2.5	49	54
Travel agents	Sales and Related	Postsecondary vocational award	L	101	102	1	1.0	7	8
Veterinary technologists and technicians	Healthcare Practitioners and Technical	Associate degree	L	71	100	29	41.0	22	51
Welders, cutters, solderers, and brazers	Production	Postsecondary vocational award	H	409	430	21	5.1	87	108
Welding, soldering, and brazing machine setters, operators, and tenders	Production	Postsecondary vocational award	H	53	54	2	3.0	11	13

Note: Numbers are in thousands.

[a]Quartile rank by 2006 median annual wages: very high (VH) more than $46,360; high (H) $30,630 to $46,300, low (L) $21,260 to $30,560, and very low (VL) less than $21,220. Information on quartile rankings is available at http://www.bls.gov/emp/empqrank.htm.

Source: http://www.bls.gov/emp/empqrank.htm.

References

Dohm, A., and Shniper, L. "Occupational Employment Projections to 2016." *Monthly Labor Review,* 2007, *130*(11), 86–125.

Employment and Training Administration. Occupational Information Network. O*NET database. 2007. Accessed Dec. 6, 2008, at http://www.onetcenter.org/database.html.

Franklin, J. "An Overview of the BLS Projections to 2016." *Monthly Labor Review,* 2007, *130*(11), 3–12.

National Center for Education Statistics. *Integrated Postsecondary Data System,* 2008. http://www.nces.ed.gov/ipeds. Table generated by author for institutions providing two-year but less than four-year programs. Certificates include less than 1 year, 1 but less than 2 year, and 2 but less than 4 year certificates.

Su, B. "The U.S. Economy to 2016: Slower Growth as Boomers Begin to Retire." *Monthly Labor Review,* 2007, *130*(11), 13–32.

Toossi, M. "Labor Force Projections to 2016: More Workers in Their Golden Years." *Monthly Labor Review,* 2007, *130*(11), 33–52.

U.S. Bureau of Labor Statistics. "Occupational Employment Statistics, May 2006." Washington, D.C.: U.S. Government Printing Office, May 2007.

U.S. Bureau of Labor Statistics. *Occupational Projections and Training Data, 2008-09 Edition.* Washington, D.C.: U.S. Government Printing Office, 2008.

U.S. Bureau of Labor Statistics. *Current Population Survey.* 2008. Accessed Dec. 6, 2008, at http://www.bls.gov/cps/home.htm#data.

Woods, R., and Figueroa, E. "Industry Output and Employment Projections to 2016." *Monthly Labor Review,* 2007, *130*(11), 53–85.

DIXIE SOMMERS *is assistant commissioner for occupational statistics and employment projections at the U.S. Bureau of Labor Statistics.*

5

This chapter highlights some of the fastest-growing occupations in the health care field that are appropriate to the community college.

The Outlook in the Health Sciences

Janell Lang

Never before has the demand for health care professionals been as great as it is now. But the supply of qualified domestic graduates is not expected to keep up with this demand, thus creating a shortage in most fields. Although the need in nursing is well documented, just as great a need exists in other health care fields: home health aides, pharmacy technicians, medical assistants, health information technologists, clinical laboratory technicians, dental hygienists, radiographers, physical therapist assistants, veterinary technologists, and health care workers who are multicredentialed.

Advances in medical technology will continue to improve the survival rate of patients who have experienced severe trauma or life-threatening diseases. This increased survival rate, coupled with the escalating numbers of baby boomers demanding quality health care services, will call for increasing numbers of professionals educated in the historical health care disciplines and in new ones just across the horizon. So in addition to the traditional associate degree programs in nursing and allied health offered by community colleges, a need exists to create short-term postsecondary programs, one-year certificate programs, and postgraduate programs leading to advanced certifications.

Changes in health care policy at the national level can have a great impact on this industry and may either increase or decrease the demand or supply in certain areas. This chapter reviews the trends in selective health care programs appropriate to the community college, assuming recent trends and policies remain in place.

NEW DIRECTIONS FOR COMMUNITY COLLEGES, no. 146, Summer 2009 © 2009 Wiley Periodicals, Inc.
Published online in Wiley InterScience (www.interscience.wiley.com) • DOI: 10.1002/cc.365

Nursing Programs

Besides the standard degree programs in nursing, a number of other credit and noncredit opportunities are of interest to the community college. Here is a brief review of some of the major nursing and related programs.

Registered Nursing. The latest projections from the U.S. Department of Labor Bureau of Labor Statistics indicate that the occupation with the largest job growth is registered nursing, with 1 million openings expected (23 percent growth rate) between 2006 and 2016 (U.S. Bureau of Labor Statistics, 2007b). New jobs will be responsible for 587,000 of those openings, with the remainder being net replacement needs (Dohm and Shniper, 2007). There are several reasons for this large demand. The aging of both the workforce and the population combines to create an increasing number of replacement needs due to retirements and, consequently, unique opportunities for educators (Franklin, 2007). In addition, for an extended period of time, many registered nurses (over 90 percent are female) leave nursing to work in a different field or leave the workforce altogether to raise their children.

According to the American Association of Community Colleges (2008), "More than 60 percent of new RNs are educated in associate's degree programs," and 79 percent of those were educated in community colleges (Viterito and Teich, 2002). Approximately 850 RN programs grant associate degrees (U.S. Bureau of Labor Statistics, 2008a). Community colleges are the educational institutions of choice for African American, Hispanic, and Native American students, and community colleges educate the majority of nurses in rural areas (Viterito and Teich, 2002).

On the supply side, a number of constraints on increasing those working in the field exist. To inaugurate an associate degree nursing program, careful and deliberate planning must occur for at least eighteen to twenty-four months before enrolling the charter class. Clinical education sites, college laboratory space and equipment, and qualified faculty must be secured. Since these programs are expensive to operate, colleges often must make difficult choices on the campus level to reallocate funds from within existing tight budgets. Additional state and local funding may be secured if a strong regional demand can be shown.

Efforts are being made in several states to raise the entry-level requirement of registered nurses to baccalaureate level or to mandate that associate degree nurses earn a bachelor's degree within an established number of years or lose their licenses. Further credentialing might be necessary for job advancement but would exacerbate existing shortages. Establishing articulation agreements with colleges and universities offering B.S.N. completion programs and A.D.N. to M.S.N. programs is critical. Although National League of Nursing-Accreditation Commission accreditation is not mandatory, it is strongly urged that community college nursing programs seek it. An argument frequently used by critics of associate degree nursing programs is that although virtually all baccalaureate degree programs are accredited by this association, only half of the associate degree programs have sought this national mark of excellence.

An important additional constraint on producing more graduates is the looming shortage of qualified nursing faculty. This may be the greatest challenge in launching or expanding a nursing program at the community college. In 2006, there were 629 RN to B.S.N. programs in the United States but only 149 RN to M.S.N. programs (U.S. Bureau of Labor Statistics, 2008d). This number needs to expand significantly if community colleges are to attract faculty in large measure by "growing their own." One of the best strategies for securing nursing faculty, staff, and administrators is to foster in students a sense of commitment to lifelong learning and to return to the learning communities in which they prospered.

Licensed Practical and Licensed Vocational Nursing Programs. Licensed practical and licensed vocational nursing (LPN/LVN) programs should be tied to local employment needs. Projected national employment to 2016 is 105,000 new openings, a 14 percent increase from 749,000 in 2006 to 854,000 in 2016 (U.S. Bureau of Labor Statistics, 2008a). Graduates of a one-year certificate program are eligible to sit for the National Council Licensure Examination for a Practical Nurse (PN-NCLEX) examination; licensure is required in all states and the District of Columbia.

Many LPNs and LVNs are employed in acute care settings such as hospitals, but the vast majority work in long-term assisted living and nursing home settings. At the same time that employment needs are being met, graduates have the prospect of continuing their education through seamless pathway programs. Furthermore, this program increases retention rates by allowing a "second chance" for students who are academically unsuccessful in the traditional registered nursing associate degree program.

RN Bridge Programs. Other types of nursing programs that community colleges may wish to consider are transition programs. Bridge programs such as the LPN to A.D.N. Progression Program allow students to build on their practical nursing knowledge and enter an accelerated associate degree track. Typically this program can be completed in three terms rather than the traditional four-term sequence. During their first semester, students enroll in bridge classes in which only the theory and skills not contained in the LPN or LVN program are taught. Then they merge with the generic or basic nursing students during the second year of the A.D.N. curriculum. Usually only two to three new courses need to be developed to offer this progression program.

Another thriving transition program is the Paramedic to RN Bridge Program, another accelerated program that takes into account the knowledge base of registered paramedics, allowing them to complete the associate degree program in three semesters. After the terrorist attacks of September 11, 2001, enrollment of paramedics in nursing programs surged. Graduates of this program possess a wealth of competencies in both the first and immediate lines of defense and at the second line: health care providers who are skilled in victim triage, isolation techniques, and immediate surgical interventions. In other words, nurses who know how to work in the field as well as on a medical/surgical unit or operating room will be at a premium.

Since the students in bridge programs merge with those in other programs, only three to four courses need to be developed for this purpose. The bridge programs are most successful when the didactic portions of the nursing curriculum, as well as the arts and sciences courses, are offered by distance learning platforms. Paramedics typically work twenty-four hours on, forty-eight hours off, so a traditional classroom-based program will not work for them. Also, clinical educational rotations need to be offered one day per week in twelve-hour shifts to accommodate their work schedules.

RN Refresher Programs. Community colleges may find great opportunities in offering nurse refresher courses for individuals who have been away from nursing for a period of time but want to return to work. These programs combine didactic portions on anatomy, physiology and pathophysiology, pharmacology, and new privacy and safety regulations, and offer a clinical rotation in which these returning nurses can attain competency in a hospital or acute care setting that has changed dramatically in the time they have been absent from the field (Dougherty, 2008).

Nurse Aide Programs. Community colleges should consider short-term certified nursing assistant (CNA) programs. They are relatively inexpensive to offer, and although certain standards must be met to satisfy state regulations, no national accreditation is mandated and the credentials of faculty are less rigorous than for those teaching in an A.D.N. Program. Jobs are also plentiful, with a projected 265,000 openings over the next ten years (U.S. Bureau of Labor Statistics, 2008b).

Home Health Aide Programs. Another rapidly growing market will be for home health aides. This field should be distinguished from another occupation with large job growth: personal and home care aides. The latter provide mainly housekeeping and personal care services, while home health aides provide assistance to patients in their homes rather than in a health care facility. Many elderly Americans are choosing to remain at home rather than receive care in nursing homes or other institutional settings, and this trend will continue. Consequently, employment numbers are expected to increase from 787,000 jobs in 2006 to 1.2 million in 2016, a 48.7 percent increase (Dohm and Shniper, 2007).

A short-term program such as a home health aide certificate will not only alleviate the acute shortage of these workers but will help community colleges fulfill their mission of access and equal opportunity to learning, especially by assisting disadvantaged students to obtain health care training.

Medical Assistant Programs

With 148,000 new job openings, amounting to an expected 35 percent increase from 2006 to 2016, medical assisting is one of the fastest-growing occupations in the country (U.S. Bureau of Labor Statistics, 2007c). These individuals work primarily in ambulatory or outpatient settings such as physicians' offices. Employment growth will be driven by the increase in the number of group practices, clinics, and other health care facilities. Fueled by advances in medical technology and the aging of the population, these agencies require a high proportion of support personnel, particularly multiskilled medical assistants who can perform both administrative and clinical procedures.

Both one-year certificate and two-year associate degree programs may be offered in this health care discipline, and although certification is not mandatory, employers favor those who are graduates of an accredited program and hold the credential of certified medical assistant (CMA). This allows the medical assistant, based on individual state law, to perform advanced clinical tasks such as administering injections, drawing blood, performing electrocardiograms, removing sutures, and changing dressings. Other opportunities arise for community colleges to offer graduates short-term specialized assistant programs in the ophthalmic, optometric, and podiatric medical assisting fields (U.S. Bureau of Labor Statistics, 2008a).

Dental Hygiene and Dental Assisting Programs

Both dental hygiene and dental assisting are listed in the BLS's "Fastest Growing Occupations, 2006–2016" (U.S. Bureau of Labor Statistics, 2007c). Employment is projected to grow 30 percent for hygienists by 2016 and 29 percent for assistants. Dental hygiene programs lead to an associate degree, and dental assistant programs may be completed through a one-year certificate program.

A few states allow dental assistants to perform any function delegated to them by the dentist. Hygienists' duties are more prescribed, and all states, with the exception of Alabama, require licensure in order to practice. Nearly all states also require graduation from an accredited program as eligibility to sit for the licensure examination.

Competition for acceptance into a dental hygiene program is fierce, with many more qualified applicants than available seats, and jobs will continue to be plentiful, with higher-than-average salaries and benefits. However, dental assistants, especially those without formal education, will have limited opportunities for advancement.

It is important to note that although opportunities abound for dental hygiene and dental assisting education, they are perhaps the most expensive programs to inaugurate and maintain. Costs of laboratory space, dental and radiography equipment, materials and supplies, and faculty salaries

NEW DIRECTIONS FOR COMMUNITY COLLEGES • DOI: 10.1002/cc

(due to stringent faculty-to-student clinical ratios and the physical presence of a dentist during all clinical laboratory sessions) are high. Partnerships with local and regional dental societies may be one avenue to sharing start-up costs, depending on geographical location and shortage of programs in that area. However, even with financial support to implement programs, expenditures of physical and human resources to maintain the operations of a dental hygiene or dental assisting clinic usually are the greatest of any health care programs offered by community colleges.

Physical Therapist Assistant Programs

Physical therapist assistant (PTA) is another occupation that ranks in the BLS's list of fastest-growing occupations between 2006 and 2016 (U.S. Bureau of Labor Statistics, 2007c). The increasing elderly population, an estimated 78 million baby boomers, is a group with much greater-than-average health care needs and will demand services to alleviate chronic and debilitating diseases. This condition, coupled with advances in medical technology that will continue to improve the survival rate of patients who have experienced severe trauma or life-threatening diseases, will call for increasing numbers of physical therapist assistants, from 60,000 jobs in 2006 to 80,000 in 2016, a 32 percent increase (U.S. Bureau of Labor Statistics, 2007c). Use of PTAs may rise even more drastically based on possible changes in Medicare and Medicaid reimbursement, which could reduce the patient cost of physical therapy services.

Nonetheless, the greatest challenge PTA programs face is faculty shortages. Although there are many physical therapists (PTs) and physical therapist assistants (PTAs) who may wish to leave clinical practice to join the teaching ranks in a community college, many will not and cannot do so due to the significant differences in salary between what community colleges can offer and what these individuals can make in the private sector. Moreover, accreditation standards mandate that while a program director may be either a PT or PTA, he or she must hold a master's degree and meet specified criteria as they relate to clinical and educational expertise and experience. Finally, with the entry-level credential for a physical therapist being raised to the clinical doctorate, it will become increasingly more difficult to recruit and retain faculty within programs at community colleges.

Clinical Laboratory and Medical Laboratory Technology Programs

Within the field of clinical laboratory sciences, excellent job opportunities exist, and more medical and clinical laboratory technicians will be needed. By 2016 twenty-three thousand new positions at the technician level will open. The volume of laboratory tests will swell with both the aging population growth and the advancement of new medical tests (U.S. Bureau of Labor Statistics, 2008a).

Tied to the knowledge of cellular structure, chemical composition, and functions of normal and abnormal tissue and the skills to prepare, fix, process, embed, section, and stain tissue, these individuals will also be highly skilled in computer technologies and baseline analyses. They may work in many areas of clinical laboratories or specialize in one specific field.

Therefore, community colleges that are planning to inaugurate an associate degree program in clinical laboratory technology (CLT) may wish to design a feeder program, such as phlebotomy, that could also be a stand-alone short-term certificate as well as a specialty area (for example, histotechnology, which is usually a twelve-month certificate program). The challenge will be securing sufficient numbers of clinical education sites, as most laboratories will take only one or two students per term.

Veterinary Technology Programs

Just as consumers will continue to demand quality health care for themselves, they will also expect a similar level of care for their pets. The BLS compares the duties a veterinary technologist performs for a veterinarian to those a nurse would for a physician (U.S. Bureau of Labor Statistics, 2008a). The projected growth in this discipline will soar from 71,000 jobs in 2006 to 100,000 in 2016, a 41 percent increase. A shortage is expected due to the relatively few two-year programs in the country (there are only 131) and the rather brief time (seven to eight years) that workers tend to remain in the field (U.S. Bureau of Labor Statistics, 2008a).

Associate degree programs must be accredited by the American Veterinary Medical Association in order for graduates to be eligible to sit for the credentialing exam. And although each state has its own rules and regulations, all require the credentialing exam in order to practice.

Most veterinary technology programs house small animals, and there are myriad U.S. Department of Agriculture rules and regulations concerning their safe and humane treatment. Human attendants must be present daily to feed, water, and exercise the animals, and a licensed veterinarian must be on call twenty-four hours per day in case of emergency. One of the most crucial decisions to make before implementing this program is to ascertain whether the community's employers will compensate these technologists with salaries commensurate with their education and training.

Pharmacy Technician Programs

A 32 percent increase in the number of pharmacy technicians is anticipated, raising employment needs from 285,000 in 2006 to 376,000 by 2016 (U.S. Bureau of Labor Statistics, 2007c). This increase is being fueled by the surging number of prescriptions an aging population needs. While these individuals work primarily in retail pharmacies and grocery stories, employment is also found in hospitals, nursing homes, and assisted-living facilities—in other words, in every practice setting where pharmacy is practiced (U.S. Bureau of Labor Statistics, 2008a).

Although there are no federal stipulations for certification and very few states mandate it, employers are much more likely to hire someone who has formal training and has been credentialed as a certified pharmacy technician (CPhT) by successfully completing the national certification examination offered by the Pharmacy Technician Certification Board. Community colleges can initiate short-term pharmacy technician certificate programs that offer didactic, laboratory, and clinical components leading to eligibility for certification.

Radiologic Technology Programs

Employment of radiographers over the next several years is projected to grow faster than average, with an estimated thirty thousand additional technologists needed by 2016 (U.S. Bureau of Labor Statistics, 2008a). The shortages in radiology are compounded by the escalating reliance on and consumer demand for medical imaging procedures. The challenge is faculty recruitment and retention: the average age of full-time professors is fifty-four, and it is anticipated that within the next few years, 27 percent of full-time and 80 percent of part-time positions will be vacant, in large part due to retirements (Rahn and Wartman, 2007).

While new programs are needed, the Joint Review Committee/Education in Radiologic Technology currently accredits radiography programs in 260 two-year colleges in the United States. These established programs should consider offering avenues for their graduates and other radiographers to further their education and earning abilities. Postgraduate programs leading to advanced certifications in computed tomography, magnetic resonance imaging, mammography, and radiation therapy can afford radiographers the opportunity to specialize and become multicredentialed. The didactic portions of these educational programs can be offered in a distance learning format, and typically the technologist's employer (primarily hospitals) allows the employee to perform clinical preceptor hours at that institution, thus not depleting the number of clinical sites for current radiography students.

Health Information Technology Programs

The field of health information technology is one of the most exciting prospects, surging with growth opportunities. These individuals are medical language experts who interpret, process, store, and retrieve health information for research and data collection. Employment in this area is projected to increase 18 percent by 2016, with thirty thousand workers needed (U.S. Bureau of Labor Statistics, 2008a). Job growth will occur, according to the BLS, "because of rapid growth in the number of medical tests, treatments, and procedures that will be increasingly scrutinized by health insurance companies, regulators, courts, and consumers" (U.S. Bureau of Labor Statistics, 2008a).

As the complexity of health care increases, other specific areas within this field have emerged as sources for careers. These include specializations in coding, transcription, and cancer registry. The shortage in cancer registry professionals will be exacerbated by the fact that the accreditation agency, the National Cancer Registrars Association (2008), has mandated that, effective 2010, the minimum entry-level requirement to become a certified tumor registrar will be an associate degree.

Conclusion

Depending on the organizational structure of community colleges and state subsidy regulations, many of the short-term certificate programs may be offered on either side of the house: academic or corporate and community service. Certificate programs, which are pathways to associate degree programs, are best offered through the academic unit.

Finally, almost all health care practitioners are required to complete an established number of continuing education hours to retain certification or licensure. There is ample room for community colleges to build on their program foundations to offer these courses. The principal challenge in this area will be application for state and national approval for awarding of continuing education hours.

Nursing and allied health programs are expensive, labor intensive, and regulated by national accreditation agencies and federal and state mandates, and they have become the flagship programs of many community colleges.

References

American Association of Community Colleges. *Keeping America Healthy and Safe.* Washington, D.C.: American Association of Community Colleges, 2008.

Dohm, A., and Shniper, L. "Occupational Employment Projections to 2016." *Monthly Labor Review,* 2007, *130*(11), 86–125.

Dougherty, C. "Slowdown's Side Effect: More Nurses." *Wall Street Journal,* May 7, 2008, p. 5.

Franklin, J. C. "An Overview of BLS Projections to 2016." *Monthly Labor Review,* 2007, *130*(11), 3–12.

National Cancer Registrars Association. "Eligibility." 2008. Accessed Aug. 10, 2008, at http://www.ctrexam.org/eligibility/index.htm#sub4.

Rahn, D. W., and Wartman, S. A. "For the Health-Care Workforce, a Critical Prognosis." *Chronicle of Higher Education,* Nov. 2, 2007, p. 8.

U.S. Bureau of Labor Statistics. "Health Technologists, Technicians, and Health Care Support Occupations." Washington, D.C.: U.S. Department of Labor, 2008a.

U.S. Bureau of Labor Statistics. "Occupations with the Largest Job Growth." 2008b. Accessed Dec. 5, 2008, at http://bls.gov/emp/emptab3.htm.

U.S. Bureau of Labor Statistics. "Fastest Growing Occupations, 2006–16." 2008c. Accessed Dec. 5, 2008, at http://bls.gov/emp/emptab21.htm.

U.S. Bureau of Labor Statistics. "Registered Nurses." 2008d. Accessed Dec. 5, 2008, at http://bls.gov/oco/ocos083.htm.

Viterito, A., and Teich, C. *The Nursing Shortage and the Role of the Community Colleges in Nurse Education.* Washington, D.C.: American Association of Community Colleges, 2002.

JANELL LANG is responsible for faculty development through Owens Community College's Center for Teaching and Learning and is a program consultant for Mercy College of Northwest Ohio.

NEW DIRECTIONS FOR COMMUNITY COLLEGES • DOI: 10.1002/cc

6

A bachelor's degree is required for many high-wage jobs, but the community college has an important role to play as an entry and reentry point for a growing number of occupations.

The Outlook in Business and Related Fields

Robert Walker

As oil prices fluctuate widely and a worldwide recession grows, we are seeing a fundamental shift in the U.S. economy and in consumer buying behavior. This shift is forcing every organization to maximize its efficiency in order to remain profitable and is thereby creating a higher demand for new staff who have management and project management experience and education (Boyd, 2008). In addition, the reduction of labor costs through overseas outsourcing and the increasing use of technology will reduce the number of domestic manufacturing workers while increasing the number of information technology and management jobs (Dohm and Shniper, 2007). Internships are becoming increasingly important for both community college and baccalaureate students as a gateway for entering the workforce (Boyd, 2008). This chapter highlights the major areas of growth in the business area and points out some of the challenges and opportunities that remain for community colleges.

Major Growth Areas

Despite current labor market difficulties, the long-term demand in critical business-related occupations remains positive. The following areas have been highlights in our analysis of the long-term labor market data provided by the Bureau of Labor Statistics.

Accountants and Auditors, Bookkeeping, Accounting, and Auditing Clerks. The U.S. Bureau of Labor Statistics (2008) projects openings

NEW DIRECTIONS FOR COMMUNITY COLLEGES, no. 146, Summer 2009 © 2009 Wiley Periodicals, Inc.
Published online in Wiley InterScience (www.interscience.wiley.com) • DOI: 10.1002/cc.366

for accountants and auditors to increase by 226,000 jobs, or 17.7 percent, between 2006 and 2016. This is due primarily to the increased number of businesses, changing financial laws and regulations, and greater scrutiny of company finances (Dohm and Shniper, 2007).

Most states require 150 semester hours of college coursework to become a certified public accountant (CPA) candidate. Community colleges can help students interested in becoming a CPA by having articulation agreements with baccalaureate institutions.

Other high-wage jobs in the accounting field usually require at least a bachelor's degree. Students at the community college who desire to enter these fields should be directed into programs and courses that prepare them for transfer.

Bookkeeping, accounting, and auditing clerk jobs are predicted to increase by 264,000 by 2016, or 12.5 percent. Most positions require a minimum of a high school diploma. However, having some college education is increasingly important, and an associate degree in business or accounting is required for some positions. Although a bachelor's degree is rarely required, community college graduates may accept positions in these fields in order to get into a particular company or to enter the accounting or finance field with the hope of eventually being promoted. Employees who meet the employer's education and work requirements can obtain a junior accounting position, which leads to accountant positions by those who demonstrate their skills (U.S. Bureau of Labor Statistics, 2008).

Personal Financial Advisors and Financial Analysts. Openings for these occupations are expected to grow by 41 percent and 33.8 percent, respectively, adding 72,000 and 75,000 jobs between 2006 and 2016 (Dohm and Shniper, 2007). These are two of the most rapid growth areas in business, but they will not produce the largest number of jobs. A bachelor's degree is not required to become a personal financial advisor, although most personal financial advisors hold licenses provided by the Financial Industry Regulatory Authority. The Series 7 license requires sponsorship, and students must maintain a relationship with a large security firm. These firms provide industry training that keep personal financial advisors abreast of the latest trends and regulations.

Financial analysts require strong communication, human relations, and selling skills. However, many personal financial advisors and most financial analysts have bachelor's degrees or higher. Again, community college students interested in this field should be looking to enroll in strong business transfer programs.

Management and Computer Systems Analysts. Jobs in these occupations are projected to increase by 149,000, with 145,000 openings projected for some high-wage computer system analyst positions by 2016 (Dohm and Shniper, 2007). Although the most common pathway into these fields is a four-year degree, the associate degree with significant experience in the field is another path of entry. Keeping current with new technology is a common requirement for these positions. Offering courses in using current technology allows community colleges to educate lifelong learners no matter what degree attainment the person has achieved. In fact, keeping current in the field and providing continued education in technologies and trends is a key for success in all business-related fields.

Entrepreneurship. In the next decade, large numbers of aging baby boomers are projected to become entrepreneurs, increasing the number of self-employed. In 2006, about 8 percent of all jobs were held by the self-employed, with 12.2 million people in this category. This is projected to increase 5.5 percent over the decade 2006 to 2016, increasing the number of self-employed by 700,000. This growth reverses a 3 percent decline in self-employment between 1996 and 2006 (Dohm and Shniper, 2007).

With large layoffs in U.S. manufacturing and downsizing in corporate America over the past few years, the media have highlighted the growth in small businesses as important generators of new jobs. As a consequence, many students who enter community colleges hope to become successful entrepreneurs.

This increased interest in entrepreneurship provides opportunities for community colleges to educate existing and returning students with entrepreneurial certificates, diplomas, and degrees. It also encourages community colleges to work with their local Small Business Development Centers, the Social Corps of Retired Executives, the Small Business Administration, and local initiatives to increase entrepreneurship and economic development. The returning students may not be interested in degree completion but will focus on gaining the knowledge needed to launch and develop their business.

Offering entrepreneurial certificates and diplomas provides structured programs of credit classes that can be promoted across the campus as an add-on to existing programs. For example, self-employed business and financial workers accounted for about 3 million jobs in 2006; the fields of art, design, entertainment, sports, and media are expected to add 60,100 self-employed jobs by 2016, and building and grounds cleaning and maintenance occupations are expected to grow by 54,000 (Dohm and Shniper, 2007).

Occupations Requiring an Associate Degree

In the BLS lexicon of occupations, very few jobs are listed as specifically requiring the associate degree. However, this does not do justice to the role that community colleges can play in providing pathways to occupations in business-related fields. Students who are interested in a bachelor's degree can be offered high-level transfer programs. A rich variety of occupations may not require a college degree, but some education at the community college level will give job seekers an advantage in difficult and competitive labor markets.

The retail sales and customer service areas, for instance, will add 557,000 and 545,000 jobs, respectively, in the period 2006 to 2016. About 50 percent of the employees in both of these areas report having some college education (Crosby and Moncarz, 2006; Dohm and Shniper, 2007). Associate degrees and certificates in management, marketing, and selling provide the additional education and endorsements needed for promotion and advancement in these fields.

Other rapidly growing areas are in executive secretary and administrative assistant positions. They are expected to add 239,000 jobs in the decade 2006 to 2016. Executive secretaries work closely with top executives. It is advantageous for these applicants to possess college degrees in the business or specific industry in which they are seeking employment.

Most secretaries, administrative assistants, receptionists, and administrative clerks acquire more advanced skills through on-the-job training. As office automation continues to evolve, retraining and continuing education will remain integral parts of secretarial, receptionist, and information clerk jobs (U.S. Bureau of Labor Statistics, 2008).

What Employers Looking Are For

In 2007, Students in Free Enterprise (2008) conducted employer surveys in seventeen cities across the United States to see what employers were looking for in college graduates compared with their perceptions of recently hired graduates. Questions addressed the importance of different characteristics in the workplace, importance of particular skill sets in the workplace, and the proficiency of graduates within skill sets. An average of 964 responded to each question; 82 percent of the respondents were from Fortune 500 companies, with 39 percent of them in the retail sector.

The largest gaps in what employers see as important versus how prepared recent graduates are were noted in the areas of problem solving and leadership, followed by communication and project management skills. The conclusion of the study is that all institutions need to better prepare students in communication, teamwork, critical thinking, and continued process improvement (systems thinking) skills.

Value of Internships

Many of the skills that business employers are looking for can be learned in the classroom. Business internships can add value to this education. Community colleges should provide internship opportunities for students, giving them experience in the field and therefore a competitive edge for job placement. Internships are often developed by using business advisory boards that keep college faculty in touch with changes in the business environment. These internships can lead to full-time employment and provide an excellent opportunity for the faculty and the business to provide invaluable feedback on students' work ethic, teamwork, communication, and human relation abilities. Internships also provide the experience needed when graduates are looking for full-time employment. Many four-year business degree programs are now requiring at least one internship experience to help teach students soft skills and the application of classroom knowledge.

Conclusion

The community college provides an entry to many growing business occupations and a reentry for those changing careers through the year 2016. The courses offered and available internships may be for specific career-oriented education or to prepare students to transfer.

With flexible curricula and closeness to business communities through their advisory boards, community colleges are well positioned to make changes as the business environment evolves. As consumer buying behavior changes and our economy adapts, it is imperative that community colleges pay close attention to trends and data to guide decisions on existing and future programs, certificates, and degrees as a service to their students and communities.

To ensure that business graduates can transfer a high percentage of their course work, articulation agreements with four-year colleges must be worked out. If these agreements are not in place, problems can arise when students seek to transfer. Some four-year business programs restrict the transfer of community college courses accepted because they classify them as junior- or senior-level courses, even though the community college may teach a very similar course. These courses could be rejected as applying toward their degrees or considered only as business electives. The Association of Collegiate Business Schools and Programs accredits associate-, baccalaureate-, and graduate degree-granting institutions. This commonality of accreditation allows for a friendly discussion for letters of articulation and greater acceptance of transfer courses at some colleges.

In working with accreditation procedures over the past few years, I have found that community colleges are increasing the number of internships required for degree completion. These colleges have to be wary of offering what the four-year college regards as a junior- or senior-level course. Although some of these courses might be necessary for occupational programs of study, students desiring transfer credit for them should be properly advised as to specific articulation agreements with four-year institutions.

References

Boyd, J. "What Employers Want: 2007 Business Professional Survey Results." Paper presented at the Annual Meeting of the Association of Collegiate Business Schools and Programs, New Orleans, La., June 2008.
Crosby, O., and Moncarz, R. "The 2004–14 Job Outlook for People Who Don't Have a Bachelor's Degree." *Occupational Outlook Quarterly,* 2006, *50*(3), 28–41.

Dohm, A., and Shniper, L. "Occupational Employment Projections to 2016." *Monthly Labor Review*, 2007, *130*(11), 86–125.

Students in Free Enterprise. "2008 Career Insights: Perspectives from the SIFE Student and Business Network." 2008. Accessed Aug. 27, 2008, at http://www.sife.org/united_states/sife_teams/hrn_pdfs/Survey_Results.pdf.

U.S. Bureau of Labor Statistics. *Occupational Outlook Handbook, 2008–09.* Washington, D.C.: U.S. Department of Labor, 2008.

ROBERT WALKER *teaches business at Kirkwood Community College in Cedar Rapids, Iowa.*

7

This chapter discusses the challenges and opportunities for students and colleges in this occupational area. Practical suggestions on how colleges can respond are offered.

The Outlook in Engineering-Related Technology Fields

Peggie Weeks

Community colleges have a long and impressive history of preparing a well-qualified technical workforce to meet the immediate and short-term needs of local and regional industries. Programs range from certificates in areas such as drafting, computer-aided design, and automotive technology to associate degrees in electrical and mechanical technologies, manufacturing, and chemical and process technologies, to name just a few.

We as a nation have made numerous attempts to define what engineering technicians do and how they differ from engineers and technologists. In some fields, technicians are being asked to assume many of the responsibilities that were once the purview of the engineer. At the same time, many engineering schools are moving away from a strictly theoretical, abstract education for engineering students toward more applications-oriented curricula. These changes are blurring the lines between technical occupations that historically may have been well defined.

In 1962, a seminal paper, "Characteristics of Excellence in Engineering Technology Education," was published (American Society for Engineering Education, 1962). Serving as the culmination of a study funded by the National Science Foundation, the paper put forth the definition of engineering technology as "that part of the engineering field which requires the application of scientific and engineering knowledge and methods combined with technical skills in support of engineering activities; it lies in the occupational area between the craftsman and the engineer at the end of the area closest to the engineer."

New Directions for Community Colleges, no. 146, Summer 2009 © 2009 Wiley Periodicals, Inc.
Published online in Wiley InterScience (www.interscience.wiley.com) • DOI: 10.1002/cc.367

More recently, the International Technology Education Association (2002) defined *technology* as "the tangible artifacts of the human-designed world (e.g., bridges, automobiles, computers, satellites, medical imaging, devices, drugs, genetically engineered plants) and the systems of which these objects are a part (e.g., transportation, communications, healthcare, food production), as well as the people, infrastructure, and processes required to design, manufacture, operate, and repair the objects" (2002, p. 7). Still others choose to look at engineering-related technologies more broadly as those occupations whose focus is on science, technology, engineering, and mathematics (STEM) disciplines. This chapter looks to the U.S. Bureau of Labor Statistics and makes some general assumptions about what constitutes engineering-related technology occupations.

Bureau of Labor Statistics Projections

In its 2006 report, the BLS listed forty engineering-related technology occupations that fall under the education and training category of either associate degree (eighteen occupations) or postsecondary award (twenty-two occupations). (The appendix in Chapter Four provides a complete list.) Fourteen of these occupations are expected to grow by 10 percent or more through 2016. The fastest-growing associate-level occupations are in computer support and environmental technologies, and the fastest-growing postsecondary award-level occupations include medical equipment repair and security system installation. Thirteen occupations have 2006–2016 growth plus net replacement need numbers greater than 25,000; among the highest numbers are for computer support specialists, welders and related occupations, and automotive service technicians and mechanics. Occupations that are expected to see a decline in growth include certain electric repairers (motor, powerhouse, and related fields), prepress technicians, and semiconductor processors.

What Tomorrow's Technicians Should Know and Be Able to Do

The Department of Labor's Occupational Information Network (O*NET) is an online database that provides information on over nine hundred occupations. For each occupation, O*NET prioritizes and describes the most important knowledge, skills, and abilities that reflect the current labor market. The information from O*NET can be used to determine the most critical attributes that employers are emphasizing in some of the high-demand technical occupations. (For those interested in what these skills cover and for free use of the database, see http://www.onetcenter.org/content.html.)

Based on the BLS data, among the occupations that will either experience growth or will have a need for significant numbers of workers in the next decade are computer support specialist, electrical engineering technician, environmental engineering technician, environmental science tech-

NEW DIRECTIONS FOR COMMUNITY COLLEGES • DOI: 10.1002/cc

nician, automotive specialty technician, security system installer, and medical equipment repairer. O*NET provides a list of the top four knowledge, skill, and ability areas for each of these seven occupations. The knowledge areas that stand out (that is, those that three or more of the seven occupations list among the top four most important) are customer and personal service, engineering and technology, computers and electronics, and English language. Although mathematics was in the top four for only one of the occupations, it was nonetheless listed as being of high importance for five of the seven occupations. The skill areas that stand out (those that three or more of the seven occupations list among the top four most important) are troubleshooting, reading comprehension, critical thinking, and active listening. The ability areas that stand out (those that three or more of the seven occupations list among the top four most important) are deductive reasoning, oral comprehension, problem sensitivity (the ability to tell when something is wrong or is likely to go wrong), and near vision (the ability to see details at close range).

Information provided in the O*NET database is helpful to colleges seeking to infuse their programs with critical marketable skills that technical students need. Another useful exercise is to develop program outcomes based on what students ought to know and be able to do. ABET, the recognized accrediting agency for college and university programs in applied science, computing, engineering, and technology, has developed guidelines that will assist community colleges in this endeavor.

Accreditation Criteria

ABET's Technology Accreditation Commission (TAC) is charged with overseeing accreditation specifically for engineering technology programs. It provides engineering technology programs with guidelines known as the Technology Accreditation Criteria (ABET, 2008). These criteria have undergone significant reform over the past decade; they are now outcomes based and far less prescriptive than before, focusing on what students learn rather than on what is taught.

Regardless of whether community college programs are TAC ABET accredited, they should be paying attention to the program outcomes criteria, known as the "a-k criteria" (Table 7.1). This is especially true for the colleges' associate degree programs in engineering-related technologies. The TAC Program Outcomes criteria, coupled with the O*NET database compendium of skill sets for given occupations, are tools that community colleges can use to design relevant programs responsive to employers' needs.

A Comprehensive Approach

Community colleges have always been aware of their multiple missions. Some schools have chosen a path that emphasizes the more academic transfer

Table 7.1. ABET Outcomes Criteria

Each program must demonstrate that graduates have:

a. An appropriate mastery of the knowledge, techniques, skills, and modern tools of their disciplines
b. An ability to apply current knowledge and adapt to emerging applications of mathematics, science, engineering, and technology
c. An ability to conduct, analyze, and interpret experiments and apply experimental results to improve processes
d. An ability to apply creativity in the design of systems, components, or processes appropriate to program educational objectives
e. An ability to function effectively on teams
f. An ability to identify, analyze, and solve technical problems
g. An ability to communicate effectively
h. A recognition of the need for and an ability to engage in lifelong learning
i. An ability to understand professional, ethical, and social responsibilities
j. A respect for diversity and a knowledge of contemporary professional, societal, and global issues
k. A commitment to quality, timeliness, and continuous improvement

Source: ABET (2008).

mission, while others focus on the vocational and training needs of their local industries. Most schools, however, have understood the importance of striking a balance between being responsive to local and regional industry needs and providing students with a broader general and technical education that will serve them no matter what career path they choose. It is this balance that will serve students best.

According to Elizabeth Teles, lead program director for the National Science Foundation's Advanced Technological Education Program, "Business and industry are demanding increased productivity per employee, multiskilled employees who can change as the jobs change, and employees with core academic and workplace skills that come to work ready but adaptable and flexible" (American Association of Community Colleges, 2005, p. v).

Challenges for Technical Education and Training

The challenges facing community colleges' engineering-related technology programs are not new. They include student preparedness, student recruitment, continuing rapid technological change, and fiscal and economic constraints.

Community colleges' open door policies have provided opportunities to millions of students who otherwise would not have even considered attending college. Nonetheless, this same policy has created challenges because many students begin their program without the prerequisite knowledge to succeed in college-level courses. Remediation continues to be the norm at virtually all community colleges. Students who enter with excitement about a particular interest in technology are often discouraged by the number of remedial courses they have to take before even setting foot in a more rigorous technical class.

Society's less-than-glamorous perception of technological occupations and careers has contributed to the challenge of recruiting students into technical community college programs. Marketing programs have had limited success, especially in recruiting women and underrepresented minorities.

The ever-increasing rate of technological change poses yet another challenge to community colleges. Ensuring that faculty stay current with the subjects they teach and that laboratory equipment is reflective of industry practice creates ongoing struggles. These struggles go hand in hand with fiscal and economic woes. Technology programs by and large are more expensive to maintain than many of the other programs on community college campuses. It is difficult for administrators to justify keeping programs with low enrollment and increasing financial needs.

Opportunities

In these challenging times, there are positive steps that community colleges can take to help their students, and the employers that ultimately hire them, achieve success. Focusing on partnerships, new funding sources, outcomes-based curricula, and true attention to diversity will foster high-quality technical programs that employers will applaud and colleges can take pride in.

Partnerships are not new. Their power emanates from the age-old idea that many hands make light (and more efficient) work. Community colleges have joined with other educational institutions and with corporate organizations to improve education for their students. Some of these partnerships are informal; others are formal agreements that capitalize on the strengths of each organization. It is imperative that colleges continue to cultivate meaningful and sustainable partnerships, especially with the stakeholders of tomorrow's high-performance workplace. Alliances with secondary schools can help high school students understand more clearly what technical programs are and what academic preparation they will need in order to enroll in a technical program of study. Student familiarity with the community college can foster strong relationships and help build their confidence.

As community colleges well know, business and industry alliances are also critical. The relationship between the corporate sector and community colleges must be seen as a win-win partnership. Corporations win because they have valuable input regarding their future workforce; colleges win because they understand what their students need to succeed in the technological workplace.

Many community colleges are typically well connected and already have strong ties with business and industry, but some schools need to move beyond industrial advisory committees and involve their industry partners in more meaningful activities. Such partnering has been the norm for many community colleges over the past fifteen years thanks to the National Science Foundation's Advanced Technological Education (ATE) program.

The ATE program, established in 1993 by Congress through the Scientific and Advanced Technology Act, promotes improvement in technician education. With an emphasis on two-year college programs, the ATE program requires that its grantees establish meaningful partnerships with business and industry in order to address current and future needs for technicians. In 2006, a survey of 163 ATE grantee institutions, many of them community colleges, revealed that the colleges were partnering with over fifty-five hundred businesses and industries, public institutions, and other educational institutions. When ATE project leaders were asked to describe best practices for partnering with industry, they cited the following: get industry involved early and be flexible; ensure persistence and a critical mass of partners; use industry experts to help with curriculum development and project evaluation; include joint membership of industry and academia on workforce development boards; focus on needs for the high-performance workplace; get decision makers involved; link company research and colleges in training of technicians; and provide flexible pathways for students (Gullickson and Wingate, 2006).

The ATE program has provided nearly eight hundred grants since 1994; over two hundred community colleges have received at least one grant, and many have received multiple awards. ATE's budget has increased steadily from $13 million to $51 million over its fifteen-year history.

While these numbers are impressive, many more community colleges could benefit. Hoping to broaden participation of the 1,157 two-year institutions, the NSF recently added a track within the ATE program: Small Grants for Institutions New to ATE. Limited to $150,000, these grants are available only to community college campuses that have not received an ATE award within the past ten years. Community colleges that have not explored funding opportunities at the NSF are now well positioned to do so. Given the current political climate and the history of ATE, it is fairly safe to say that the program will continue into the foreseeable future.

It is relatively easy to take a textbook and prepare lesson plans that reflect a certain body of knowledge. It is an altogether different matter to determine student outcomes and facilitate student learning based on those outcomes. It is especially challenging to integrate certain professional and technical skills. Educators need to find ways to incorporate skill building in these areas in the classroom. For example, consider troubleshooting, one of the critical skill areas. Do technical faculty teach this? If so, how do they teach it, and what are the outcomes? How do instructors know that a student is proficient in troubleshooting? There are no easy answers, but colleges wishing to optimize their technical programs must grapple with such issues.

When high-level administrators at the community college are asked what they are doing to attract and retain a more diverse student population, they usually speak in generalities about how they value diversity and how their institution is making strides in this area. Specific strategies for recruiting women and underrepresented minorities into technical fields are well documented, yet many of the nation's two-year colleges are not doing all they can to entice students into their technical classrooms. For example, engineering service-learning projects—projects that tie engineering to the community—see the participation of two to three times as many women as compared to the base populations in their fields (Jamieson, 2007). Could integrating service-learning and community-based projects into community college technical classes attract more women? Might it also entice more adult learners and minorities? Investigating programs such as award-winning Engineering Projects in Community Service (EPICS) might be a worthwhile first step. EPICS, which began at Purdue University in 1995, has reached over two thousand undergraduate students and now offers EPICS High to secondary students. Models like this can be adapted for technical classes at the community college level (Purdue University, 2008).

Conclusion

Community colleges will continue to have a responsibility to provide students with the education and training needed to succeed in the competitive workplace. To do that, they must continue to keep their fingers on the pulse of their local and regional industries. Their responsiveness to the needs of these industries will determine in large part whether their students succeed. These colleges also have a responsibility to prepare students for a broad range of occupations and careers by providing them with a foundational education. Doing less would be a disservice to all stakeholders.

References

ABET. "Criteria for Accrediting Engineering Technology Programs, 2008–2009." 2008. Accessed Dec. 6, 2008, at http://www.abet.org.

American Association of Community Colleges. *Advancing Technological Education: Keeping America Competitive*. Washington, D.C.: American Association of Community Colleges, 2005.

American Society for Engineering Education. "Characteristics of Excellence in Engineering Technology Education." 1962. Accessed Dec. 6, 2008, at http://www.engtech.org/docs/characteristics_of_excellence.pdf.

Gullickson, A. R., and Wingate, L. A. "The National Science Foundation's Advanced Technology Education Program Final Evaluation Report." Kalamazoo: Evaluation Center, Western Michigan University, 2006.

International Technology Education Association. *Technically Speaking: Why All Americans Need to Know More About Technology*. Washington, D.C.: National Academies Press, 2002.

Jamieson, L. "Engineering Education in a Changing World." Keynote address at the International Engineering Consortium, Sao Paulo, December 2007.
Purdue University. "Engineering Projects in Community Service." 2008. Accessed Dec. 6, 2008, at http://epics.ecn.purdue.edu/.

PEGGIE WEEKS is an industry/educational consultant with seventeen years of teaching experience in community colleges.

NEW DIRECTIONS FOR COMMUNITY COLLEGES • DOI: 10.1002/cc

8

*The community college is becoming increasingly impor-
tant in the protective service fields as a screening device
and for the skills and knowledge taught.*

The Outlook in the Protective
Service Fields

Gregory Talley, Susan Korsgren

Typically when people think of the protective service or public safety field,
they think in terms of jobs in which employees wear uniforms and report
to duty with a gun, fire hose, or first-aid kit. This is partially true of the
operational side of public safety, but this view ignores an equally important
support system that consists largely of nonsworn, or civilian, personnel
whose jobs facilitate the work of those who spend their time investigating
crimes, arresting criminals, putting out fires, and bandaging wounds.

This chapter deals primarily with the sworn positions in public safety,
in particular traditional and emerging law enforcement roles. But public
safety also relies heavily on people with technical skills that fall outside the
realm of criminal justice. For example, every agency needs people with
expertise in administrative functions such as planning and budgeting. Larger
public safety agencies hire civilian personnel to perform these functions, as
well as those who are computer technicians, mechanics, lawyers, and
researchers. There are also opportunities for crime scene and crime lab technicians, positions found in larger police departments or federal agencies; in
some cases, they require advanced degrees. Correctional facilities also hire
credentialed psychologists and psychiatrists, doctors, nurses, nurse practitioners, social workers, librarians, dietitians, pharmacists, dentists, and
clergy.

There are many opportunities in the sworn positions in the criminal
justice field. For example, most people think of police as coming in two
varieties: those who wear uniforms and drive police cars with lights and

NEW DIRECTIONS FOR COMMUNITY COLLEGES, no. 146, Summer 2009 © 2009 Wiley Periodicals, Inc.
Published online in Wiley InterScience (www.interscience.wiley.com) • DOI: 10.1002/cc.368

sirens and those who wear street clothes or suits and ties and are referred to as detectives or investigators. There also are opportunities for employment with railroad police, port authority police, waterfront police, housing authority police, and transportation police. On the federal side of law enforcement, there are opportunities to work not only with the FBI but also with the Secret Service; U.S. Marshal; Bureau of Alcohol, Tobacco and Firearms; Border Patrol; Immigration and Customs Enforcement; Federal Protective Service; Drug Enforcement Administration; and some little-known federal law enforcement agencies that are embedded within departments of the federal government. These include postal inspectors; Park Service and Forest Service rangers; and others who work for the Department of Energy, State Department, or Department of Agriculture. Most of the federal law enforcement positions, though, require at least a bachelor's degree, and some require a graduate degree. Community college students who desire careers in most of these areas should be encouraged to transfer into baccalaureate programs.

Law Enforcement Jobs

Typical entry-level requirements for a job in law enforcement on the state or local level are a high school diploma, good physical and medical condition, good hearing and eyesight, and some type of entrance or civil service exam, as well as a physical agility test, polygraph exam, psychological screening, and background investigation. Most police departments require applicants to be twenty-one years old at the time of employment to meet legal requirements to carry a handgun. Once hired, police recruits must graduate from a police academy to meet state police officer standards and training requirements. These academies range in length from about three months to upward of a year. The academy is generally followed by an assignment with a field training officer for several months. This officer ensures that the police recruit is familiar with department policies and procedures and can successfully manage a day on the job alone.

Recruits entering law enforcement routinely begin as patrol officers, who are to policing what internists are to medicine. Patrol officers are expected to have limited expertise in a wide range of skills, knowledge, and ability. The job description in the *Summary Report for Police Patrol Officers* by O*NET is quite accurate and reflects many of the job duties outlined by Sir Robert Peel in establishing the London Metropolitan Police in 1829. It is critically important that police officers have a good understanding of statutory and constitutional law. The job requires an ability to communicate with people from all walks of life, exercise good judgment in the decision-making process, and have effective written and oral communication skills. Critical thinking is extremely important in the job.

Handcuffs and handguns will probably always be tools of the trade, but the ability of police to effectively communicate their investigations and findings as well as the actions of others is a much bigger part of the job. Computers are a big part of police work today and are often mounted in patrol cars next to heads-up displays and radar and laser speed monitoring devices and video recording, license plate scanning, and infrared imaging equipment. None of this equipment is of value if officers do not know how to use it, and they must be familiar not just with the mechanics of the equipment but how it can be integrated into good old-fashioned police work. These tools, especially the data analysis capability of the computer, have helped police departments shift from an era of random patrol to directed patrol and from report takers to problem solvers. Police training programs and academies are well equipped to train police in the techniques for using these tools, but the community college is better suited for teaching the integration of the information gained with these tools into problem solving.

Protective Services Education

The often-referenced President's Commission on Law Enforcement and Administration of Justice of 1967 states that, in part, the way to improve policing is to improve the education of the police (Fagin, 2003; Bohm and Haley, 2008; Goldstein, 1990; Buerger, 2004). Consequently, the federal government poured millions of dollars into the Law Enforcement Education Program in the late 1960s and 1970s, which resulted in hundreds of criminal justice college programs springing up across the nation. Today nearly thirteen hundred colleges and universities support criminal justice programs of some type (U.S. College Search, 2008).

Clearly, educational opportunities in criminal justice abound in the United States, and courses in criminal justice can be taken at many local community colleges or online through distance education. But of the nearly thirteen thousand local police departments across the country, only 17 percent have required some college or a two-year college degree as an entrance requirement. Of the three thousand sheriffs' departments in the United States, 14 percent have required some college or a two-year degree (U.S. Bureau of Justice Statistics, 2006). Although these statistics represent official hiring practices of police and sheriffs' departments, it is important to remember that most police departments generally do not hire people under the age of twenty-one, and they require that future employees between the ages of eighteen and twenty-one be working either full time or part time while waiting for an opportunity to become a sworn police officer or attend college. Police administrators often use college attendance as a screening tool to choose between otherwise equally qualified candidates for a police job even though college attendance is not an official requirement for employment.

Colleges looking to pump graduates of criminal justice programs into police departments need to understand the resistance on the part of the long-time police officers to admit that college-educated police officers are beneficial to the department. However, as incumbent police officers retire and additional college-educated officers take to the ranks of law enforcement, college degrees will become more accepted by those in the field.

Finally, many police departments are requiring various levels of college education for promotion to supervisory positions and special assignments. Because of the nature of police work (rotating shifts and days off), it is difficult to obtain that education while on the job unless it is completed through distance education. Most police recruits do not think in terms of promotion, but having the education in advance of the job instead of getting it on the job is a bonus.

Job Growth in the Protective Services Sector

Protective service job titles include firefighters, bailiffs, correctional officers and jailers, detectives and criminal investigators, police and sheriff's patrol officers, animal control workers, and security guards, and account for nearly 3.2 million jobs. The U.S. Bureau of Labor Statistics (BLS) projects a 14.3 percent increase in new jobs in protective services, or 453,000 new jobs, from 2006 to 2016. Overall, this translates into 1.3 million new and replacement jobs during this ten-year span (Dohm and Shniper, 2007).

Job classifications with the greatest potential for entry-level positions in the protective services are for firefighters, correctional officers and jailers, sheriff's and police patrol officers, and security guards, with a total of 947,000 new and replacement jobs (Dohm and Shniper, 2007).

Firefighters. Similar to police departments, fire departments by and large require only a high school diploma as a minimum requirement for entrance, but candidates for the job are learning that they can boost their chances of getting a firefighting job by having an associate or bachelor's degree. About 368 community colleges and four-year colleges and universities offer degrees in fire science (U.S. College Search, 2008).

There were approximately 293,000 municipal firefighters in 2006, with a median wage of about $41,000 (Employment and Training Administration, 2007). Job growth is expected at 12.1 percent between 2006 and 2016, with an anticipated 142,000 new and replacement jobs (U.S. Bureau of Labor Statistics, 2008). Most job growth will take place as volunteer firefighting positions convert to paid positions in growing suburban areas and as vacancies are filled from the ranks of those who retire or change careers (Firelink, 2008).

Correctional Officers and Jailers. Job growth in the corrections industry is expected to be better than average from 2006 to 2016, with approximately 175,000 new and replacement jobs (U.S. Bureau of Labor Statistics, 2008). The median wage for a correctional officer or jailer was about $36,000 in 2006.

Many correctional facilities require only a high school degree for entry-level positions and then require completion of a preservice training program along with on-the-job training; however, some agencies are beginning to require at least some college (American Correctional Association, 2001).

Police and Detectives. Police and detectives held about 760,000 jobs in 2006. Local governments employed 79 percent of these officers, state police agencies about 11 percent, and various federal agencies about 7 percent. Employment of police officers is expected to grow 11 percent between 2006 and 2016 (Dohm and Shniper, 2007). Sheriff's deputies will also increase by 11 percent during this period, and the number of detectives will increase by 17 percent, from 106,000 in 2006 to 125,000 in 2016. It should be noted, however, that the job of a detective or investigator is not an entry-level position but a job that is acquired after years of service with a police department. Still, there will be an anticipated 243,000 new and replacement jobs in policing by 2016 (Dohm and Shniper, 2007).

Police officers and sheriff's deputies had median annual earnings of $47,460 in 2006. This same year, median annual earnings of police and detective supervisors were $69,310, and median annual earnings of detectives and investigators were $58,260 (Employment and Training Administration, 2007). Federal officers receive law enforcement availability pay equal to 25 percent of the agent's grade in step. This is awarded because of the large amount of overtime these agents are expected to work. For example, an agent's base pay may be $48,159, but in 2006, agents earned an average of $60,199 with availability pay (U.S. Bureau of Labor Statistics, 2008).

Security Guards. Growth in the security industry overshadows all the other occupations in the protective services field. The BLS (2008) estimates that this industry will grow by nearly 17 percent to a workforce that will include 387,000 new and replacement positions. These jobs typically require a high school education or general educational development credential along with on-the-job training. Some states, such as New York, require a short preservice training session along with prescribed training following employment. This training may be conducted by the employer but is also suitable for inclusion in a college's continuing or community education program. The median salary for a security guard in 2006 was $21,500 (Employment and Training Administration, 2007).

The need for security guards will increase as a result of an aging population moving to gated communities and as business, government, and industry seek to enhance asset protection. As the role of the security guard changes to that of a protection specialist, with its accompanying reliance on new technologies, we can expect to see more people move into this field as a target career.

Emergency Medical Technician and Paramedic. Paramedic and emergency medical technician (EMT) functions are closely aligned with fire departments and usually respond to calls for service when fire departments are dispatched. In fact, many fire departments employ EMTs and paramedics, who are considered part of the firefighting team. They become in essence a specialized subset of the firefighting community, and their numbers can be expected to grow as the population ages.

Generally a high school diploma is required to enter a training program to become an EMT or paramedic. Workers must complete a formal training and certification process. Most commonly the training is conducted in community colleges over one to two years and may result in an associate degree. Such education prepares the graduate to take the National Registry of Emergency Medical Technicians (NREMT) examination and become certified as a paramedic. Extensive course work and clinical field experience are required. Refresher courses and continuing education are required for EMTs and paramedics at all levels, and community colleges have a role to play in this area.

EMTs and paramedics held about 201,000 jobs in 2006. Employment is expected to grow by 19 percent, which is faster than average for all occupations. Median annual earnings of EMTs and paramedics in May 2006 were $27,070, with about 10 percent earning $45,280. Earnings will depend on geographical location, level of certification, and employment setting.

Federal Law Enforcement

Though many of the federal law enforcement jobs in the nearly one hundred departments and agencies require at least a bachelor's degree, there are many opportunities for those holding only a high school diploma or additional training and education (Walker, Burns, Bumgarner, and Bratina, 2008). In many cases, a combination of experience and education may be substituted for education. For example, the U.S. Marshals Service and Border Patrol Agents of the Customs and Border Protection Agency of the Department of Homeland Security may accept a combination of education and experience in lieu of a bachelor's degree. The Army Criminal Investigation has a minimum requirement of sixty credit hours for the nonpromotable rank of sergeant. Those in the higher ranks and civilian personnel are required to have at least a bachelor's degree. Special agents with the Secret Service are required to have a bachelor's degree, but members of the uniformed division of the Secret Service are required to have only a high school education.

The greatest opportunity for employment with the Department of Homeland Security is as a transportation security officer, otherwise known as a screener. No education beyond a high school diploma is required for these positions, though newly hired employees must complete 56 to 72 hours of classroom training, another 112 to 128 hours of on-the-job training, and then initial certification testing.

Postsecondary Education

DeLone (2008) notes that the emerging roles in policing go beyond traditional peacekeeping models and that change in policing, regardless of how slow it may move, is being driven by the events and activities taking place in the broader social context. Most notable are the changes that have been adopted by police agencies following the terrorist attacks of September 11, 2001. These changes are taking place not only in the police community but also in the firefighting, security, corrections, and paramedic fields. The paradox is that the people working in the protective services fields are the ones who must make critical decisions, often life-and-death decisions, in a few seconds or less, and these are the employees who have the least amount of training and education. Meanwhile, those who manage these organizations and often have days and weeks to make decisions are required to have baccalaureate and advanced degrees.

Wimshurst and Ransley (2007) see higher education in policing as necessary for professional standing and as a means of enabling police to cope with the complex demands of today's law enforcement. They also note that a postsecondary education should focus on analysis of current social issues, critical thinking, and problem solving. Surely today's "salad bowl," instead of "melting pot," view of the United States requires those in the protective services field to become acquainted with customs and cultures that are as unfamiliar as the languages that immigrants bring with them.

Buerger (2004) notes that three levels of qualifications have emerged for employment in policing over the years. The first level is the completion of a high school diploma accompanied with police academy training. The second level is the associate degree in criminal justice, which in some states doubles as the police academy or at least provides the classroom instruction portion of the academy training. The third level is found in four-year colleges and universities and focuses more on research than skills.

There are fundamental differences between training and education, though there is room for overlap. Training in the protective services field focuses on how to get the job done. Education's focus is on why the job is done. Both education and training focus on what is to be done, though from different perspectives. Buerger (2004) states that the work of the college and the work of the academy should complement each other and that a college education should build within students the ability to critically assess new situations and undertake new learning and question facts.

For the community college, the challenges in designing a program and improving student success are familiar ones. Many students arrive needing remedial work, and the length of the programs discourages them and leads to high dropout rates. On the curricular level, there must be a balance of the needs of students who want to transfer to a four-year program with those seeking immediate employment. In addition to recruiting faculty with theoretical backgrounds in the subjects they will be teaching, it is important to have students find someone in the classroom who has experience working in the field.

Buerger (2004) presents an interdisciplinary model in which criminal justice programs might require a specified number of hours in accounting, computer science, ethnic studies, and multiculturalism in addition to the social science core of criminal justice. If the old concern that "the new kids don't know how to talk with people" remains, then programs might consider including drama classes, public speaking, or even courses in social work that require students to interact with others.

Conclusion

Opportunities abound for prospective employees in the protective services. On the surface, it appears that few employers require a college education as a condition of employment at the state or local level. But the reality is that many employers use at least some college as a screening tool for prospective employees. Although the federal government requires a bachelor's degree for many of the investigative positions, some agencies consider a combination of education and experience, while other federal agencies require an associate degree. Community colleges are best poised to provide future police officers, firefighters, corrections officers, and security personnel with critical thinking and problem-solving skills. This is especially true in view of the fact that many of these jobs require the new employee to be at least twenty-one years old, and the community college experience provides an academic segue into these professions.

References

American Correctional Association. "Staff Education." *Corrections Compendium,* 2001, 26(2), 8–23.

Bohm, R. M., and Haley, K. N. *Introduction to Criminal Justice.* (5th ed.) New York: McGraw-Hill, 2008.

Buerger, M. "Education and Training the Future Police Officer." *FBI Law Enforcement Bulletin,* 2004, 73(1), 26–32.

DeLone, G. J. "Law Enforcement Mission Statements Post-September 11th." *Police Quarterly,* 2008, 10(2), 218–235.

Dohm, A., and Shniper, L. "Occupational Employment Projections to 2016." *Monthly Labor Review,* 2007, 130(11), 86–125.

Employment and Training Administration. *Occupational Information Network.* Raleigh, N.C.: National Center for O*NET Development, 2007.

Fagin, J. A. *Introduction to Criminal Justice.* Needham Heights, Mass.: Allyn and Bacon, 2003.

Firelink. 2008. http://edu.firelink.policelink.com/.

Goldstein, H. *Problem-Oriented Policing.* New York: McGraw-Hill, 1990.

O*NET. *Summary Report for Police Patrol Officers.* Accessed May 4, 2009, at http://online.onetcenter.org/link/summary/33-3051.01.

U.S. Bureau of Justice Statistics. *Sourcebook of Criminal Justice Statistics Online.* Washington, D.C.: U.S. Department of Justice, 2006. Accessed Dec. 6, 2008, at http://www.albany.edu/sourcebook.

U.S. Bureau of Labor Statistics. *Occupational Outlook Handbook, 2008–2009.* Washington, D.C.: U.S. Department of Labor, 2008.

U.S. College Search. "Criminal Justice Colleges and Criminal Justice Schools." Accessed Dec. 6, 2008, at http://www.uscollegesearch.org/criminal-justice-colleges.html.

U.S. College Search. "Firefighting Colleges and Firefighting Schools." Accessed Dec. 6, 2008, at http://www.uscollegesearch.org/firefighting-colleges.html.

Walker, J. T., Burns, R. G., Bumgarner, J., and Bratina, M. P. "Federal Law Enforcement Careers: Laying the Groundwork." *Journal of Justice Education,* 2008, *19*(1), 110–131.

Wimhurst, K., and Ransley, J. "Police Education and the University Sector: Contrasting Models from the Australian Experience." *Journal of Criminal Justice Education,* 2007, *18*(1), 106–122.

GREGORY TALLEY *is dean of business and public services at Broome Community College in Binghamton, New York, and a retired deputy police chief.*

SUSAN KORSGREN *is an associate professor of criminal justice at Broome Community College in Binghamton, New York, and a former U.S. Army major in the Military Police Corps.*

9

The future of noncredit workforce education programs looks bright but organizational, funding, and accountability issues remain.

The Outlook for Noncredit Workforce Education

Michelle Van Noy, James Jacobs

Postsecondary noncredit education has become increasingly common, and at many community colleges, noncredit education enrolls more students than credit programs do (Bailey and others, 2003). Much of the growth has occurred in courses connected with workforce instruction and contract training. These programs are noted for their important role in responding to shifting workforce demands and providing skills in a way that is flexible and responsive to employer needs (Dougherty and Bakia, 1999; U.S. Government Accountability Office, 2004). This growth raises fundamental questions about whether the colleges are keeping pace with student and workforce needs, using resources efficiently in their organizational approach, and providing access to all students. To explore these issues, this chapter focuses on the following questions: What is the current system of noncredit workforce education in terms of state funding policy, community college organizational practice, and program outcomes? What are current issues and future trends for noncredit workforce education?

This chapter draws on information from a study conducted in 2007 and 2008 by the Community College Research Center at Columbia University in conjunction with the National Council on Workforce Education and the National Council on Continuing Education and Training (Van Noy and others, 2008). The study used two key sources of data. First, state policies on the funding and regulation of noncredit workforce education were reviewed in all fifty states by interviewing individuals in a variety of state departments with oversight for community colleges or workforce development, or both.

NEW DIRECTIONS FOR COMMUNITY COLLEGES, no. 146, Summer 2009 © 2009 Wiley Periodicals, Inc.
Published online in Wiley InterScience (www.interscience.wiley.com) • DOI: 10.1002/cc.369

Second, case studies of twenty community colleges in ten states were conducted by interviewing key administrative staff at each college. The colleges were selected to reflect innovative practices in noncredit workforce education, as well as a range of institutional sizes, locations, and states.

The Current State of Noncredit Workforce Programs

Through noncredit workforce education, community colleges provide a wide range of short-term training. For the colleges in our case study, common noncredit programs included those in allied health, information technology, and business areas and ranged from entry level to more advanced training. In addition to these common areas, other programs included real estate, manufacturing, construction, nonprofit management, veterinary training, child care, and teacher training. Program offerings are often driven by state and local employer and labor market demands. Colleges varied in whether they decided to offer a course in a noncredit rather than credit format, depending on a complicated set of factors including state funding, labor market needs, institutional practices, and instructional approaches. To fully understand the current landscape of noncredit workforce education requires an examination of its funding sources, colleges' organizational approaches, and the recorded outcomes it generates.

Funding Sources. Funding for noncredit workforce education from state general funds provides an important signal about the state's vision for community colleges and short-term training. State general funds are those provided by the state directly to community colleges and can be used to support noncredit workforce education (Warford, 2002). As of our review in mid-2007, twenty-eight states provide funding for noncredit education through state general funds, but the various funding methods differ in their potential implications for community college programs. These states generally use one of three funding methods: a formula that includes student contact hours, a fixed amount of funding, and bundled funds that allow college discretion.

Eleven states, including Texas, California, and Maryland, provide funding using contact hours as the primary source for determining allocations using similar mechanisms as credit programs, based on student enrollments and seat time in the classroom. This type of funding strategy provides the most clearly defined and dependable source of funding, which could encourage programs to become more institutionalized at the colleges. Seven states, including Virginia and New Mexico, provide a fixed amount of funds, whereby the state provides a set allocation each year dedicated to noncredit workforce education. This funding is often small relative to the amount of funding that the state provides for credit programs and is prone to fluctuations based on the state's overall yearly budget. Ten states, including Kentucky and Michigan, bundle the funding with college discretion; that is, the state provides general funding to the colleges and allows them to decide whether to use some of the funds to support noncredit workforce education. Thus, the amount of state funds used for noncredit workforce education may vary among each of the colleges in the state.

The remaining twenty-two states, which do not provide funding, report that their college's noncredit workforce education is self-supporting through course charges to students and employers and other grants. Colleges in these states pursue a range of strategies to support noncredit workforce education, including entrepreneurial efforts, higher tuition levels, and increased pursuit of grants. Alternatively, they may simply devote fewer resources to noncredit workforce education or offer more courses in a credit mode that they would otherwise prefer to offer in a noncredit mode.

Previous studies have demonstrated that nearly all states have some type of workforce training funds for the training of workers for business and industry (Boswell, 2000; Simon, 1999). They are often designated for workforce development in targeted industries and for recruiting new employers into the state as part of incentive packages offered to businesses. In thirty-five states, training funds directly specify the community college as the fiscal agent or the preferred training provider. This specification provides a greater chance that the funds will support community college noncredit programs, often through customized training. In fact, these funds may be a central source of support for community colleges in states that do not provide general funds for noncredit education, but specify community colleges as the preferred training providers or fiscal agents.

Noncredit workforce education is often supported by charges with little regulation. Only eight states reported some type of limit on the amount that can be charged for noncredit workforce education. Several state policymakers specifically reported that colleges charge what the market will bear for noncredit courses. Limits on noncredit charges have important implications for colleges in operating noncredit programs, as lower costs will make these programs more accessible to low-income individuals for short-term training and potentially support efforts to promote access to longer-term education through noncredit education. At the same time, the goal of revenue generation is common, as many case study college noncredit programs are, or plan to become, self-supporting or profit generating in the context of limited funding. Important decisions must be made by colleges in balancing the potentially competing goals of seeking profit from noncredit courses and promoting student access and community outreach.

Organizational Approaches. In balancing the variety of needs served by noncredit workforce education, colleges have a range of organizational approaches to the management of noncredit workforce education. Issues may include organizational structures (where programs are located and how they are administered within the college) and organizational practices (how programs operate in relationship to other programs in the college). A separate organizational structure exists when noncredit workforce education is considered a distinct organizational unit within the college; an integrated organizational structure exists when noncredit workforce education is interspersed across the college's academic units by content area.

In our case study, colleges with integrated and separate organizational structures employed different practices to pursue an integrated organizational approach that would facilitate relationships between noncredit and credit programs, as well as between noncredit programs and employers. Noncredit programs with separate organizational structures coordinated their activities through regular meetings and communication throughout the college to encourage collaboration, avoid duplication, and allow movement between noncredit and credit programs as appropriate. Noncredit programs with integrated organizational structures had an organizational entity to conduct entrepreneurial outreach, maintain flexibility, and act as a central point of contact with employers. An integrated organizational approach connects noncredit programs to the rest of the college through collaboration and coordination.

The lessons from the colleges in our case study demonstrate that no single right way exists to organize noncredit workforce education; rather, a range of organizational structures and practices can promote an integrated approach. To determine which organizational structure and practices best suit a college depends on multiple factors, including college leadership, administration, and funding sources, as well as the student, employer, and community needs the college seeks to meet. However, the case study colleges provide examples of integrated organizational approaches at innovative institutions, suggesting that other colleges may benefit from considering these approaches. Several case study colleges have recently changed the organization of noncredit education to consolidate programs, elevate noncredit education, and promote workforce development. The role of noncredit workforce education is evolving, and its evolution may prompt changes in colleges' organizational approach.

Recorded Outcomes. Since noncredit workforce education is not regulated by the academic rules that govern credit education, the recorded student outcomes from participating in a noncredit program vary widely. Understanding the range of outcomes from noncredit workforce education helps illuminate how well the programs fulfill their goals. Furthermore, the mechanisms that states and colleges use to track noncredit student data and the outcomes of noncredit workforce education have implications for assessing the effectiveness of the various noncredit programs.

Noncredit programs may yield different forms of recorded outcomes to students, including a range of industry certification and licensures, transcripts, and continuing education units (CEUs). While our case study colleges offer a range of industry certifications, these programs often represent only a fraction of their total noncredit offerings. The colleges typically offer numerous noncredit workforce programs that do not have industry certifications associated with them. Nine states have different guidelines for including noncredit courses on a transcript to provide students with a

NEW DIRECTIONS FOR COMMUNITY COLLEGES • DOI: 10.1002/cc

record of course completion, and several states are considering the development of a policy on transcripts for noncredit courses. Although the majority of states do not have guidelines on transcripts for noncredit courses, individual colleges may decide to develop their own policies. CEUs are a standard way to measure participation in continuing education overseen by various associations and professional organizations. Much of the use of CEUs is industry driven, based on demand to meet the needs of particular industries such as nursing, teaching, and the law, where CEUs are required to maintain licensure.

Some concern exists over developing career pathways for students that would facilitate their movement to longer-term educational opportunities while also connecting them with employment opportunities (Alssid and others, 2002; Morest, 2006). To this end, seventeen states have policies pertaining to the retroactive granting of credit. Many of our case study colleges have guidelines that could facilitate the retroactive granting of credit for noncredit courses, such as credit for prior learning or life experience credit; however, their use by students is rare due to low interest or unfamiliarity. In addition, guidelines for articulating noncredit and credit programs may create stronger connections between the two that could allow students to move between programs in a seamless way, potentially gaining credit for noncredit courses. Increasingly, states and case study colleges were considering ways that short-term training could connect to longer-term educational opportunities.

In light of the wide range of populations potentially engaged in noncredit workforce education, standard data are needed to understand their goals and needs. While thirty-eight states require community colleges to report some information on their noncredit programs, they most typically collect data only on the total number of students enrolled. Several state policymakers have expressed concern that the data collected under existing reporting requirements undercount the number of students enrolled in noncredit workforce education. In states without reporting requirements, colleges rarely collect noncredit data for their own purposes.

Future Trends in Noncredit Workforce Education

The examination of current state and community college practices in noncredit workforce education illuminates some likely future trends. More generally, community college workforce education may face a potentially uncertain future due to changes in employer demand, changes in state support, and the rise of new competitors in for-profit institutions (Jacobs and Dougherty, 2006). However, research indicates that although these issues persist, noncredit workforce education appears to have a strong outlook. Programs will face growth and change as they continue to meet the needs of individuals, employers, and the economy at large.

Continued Growth. Based on current trends in noncredit workforce education, continued expansion of noncredit programs in a wide range of occupational areas, including both entry-level training and advanced professional training, is likely. Colleges that already have programs will likely continue to grow as individuals seek more ongoing training to keep their skills marketable in the ever-changing workplace. Advanced professional training is likely to continue in some established areas like information technology and teaching and continue to grow in other areas such as business and health care. Entry-level training will have continued importance in helping underprepared students gain occupational skills, with the potential to help them develop skills that allow movement to credit programs. Community colleges serve an important training function for a range of occupations that require short-term training or postsecondary vocational awards. These growing occupational areas are important to the economy, and community colleges provide an important entrée for workers into these occupations. However, potentially limited resources to fund noncredit workforce education for individuals are an issue that states and local areas will need to address.

Funding Uncertainties. The future of financial support for this type of noncredit workforce education is of crucial importance. Given the recent growth in noncredit programs, state systems of support are still evolving in order to fully address the needs of the range of workers who pursue short-term training and their employers, as well as the local economy. Continued growth and expansion of profit-driven noncredit programs are likely in many community colleges, and this trend may be spurred by a lack of state funding. In this context, it is important for colleges to make the case for noncredit training that contributes to opportunity for underprepared populations or promotes specific economic development objectives of the state. It is also important for colleges to balance these objectives and maintain their unique ability to move people into credit programs, particularly in the context of the increased significance of college education.

Connecting Noncredit and Credit. While noncredit workforce education will expand, colleges will need to adjust to different needs and demands from employers and individual students. In particular, with some employers and many individuals seeking degrees and credentials, colleges may need to address how to blend the two modes of learning and allow flexible, transferable forms of learning that address both short-term training needs and longer-term educational needs. Our case study colleges show that this approach is possible. However, they raise issues for colleges in terms of their organization and degree of collaboration internally. It is likely that more colleges will need to address these concerns and will look for successful models for how to articulate noncredit and credit programs and organizational approaches to best support these efforts. Likewise, states will seek models of these approaches. Several case study colleges reported that they are exploring the development of collegewide policies on life experience credits rather than courses or department-specific policies. These types of guidelines are rare, but many state policymakers reported that their states are discussing or developing guidelines to articulate noncredit programs with credit programs as a possible strategy to support the development of career pathways.

Multiple issues must be balanced in determining an approach to connect short-term training with longer-term educational programs. As colleges develop ways to articulate between noncredit and credit programs, they also need to address issues of remediation as students seek to bring their skills up to required levels to enroll in degree programs. To this end, contextualized adult education classes that combine technical workforce and basic skills offer an alternative approach to address these skills needs while providing workforce skills (Leibowitz and Taylor, 2004). As noncredit programs focus on professional and high-technology fields that value credentials, such as information technology and health care, the importance of carefully considering both the short- and longer-term educational needs increases. Policies may help support the progression of students along career pathways, but they must also be mindful of potential concerns over quality and accreditation.

Accreditation Concerns. The convergence of noncredit and credit programs is eventually going to lead to more attention by accreditation agencies to the issues of noncredit education. To date, only the Middle States Commission has specifically addressed this issue in community colleges. Others will likely need to follow suit as connections between noncredit and credit become stronger in some areas. At the same time, continued growth of noncredit in ways that are not connected with credit programs for the college raises questions for accreditation agencies about the overall quality of these programs offered under the name of the community college.

Increased Focus on Data. The lack of data on noncredit workforce education has been well documented (Voorhees and Milam, 2005). However, our study indicates that states may be moving in the direction of requiring more data and reporting from community colleges. Particularly, to the extent that accreditation agencies begin to focus on noncredit, states and colleges may also pay more attention and track more information on the characteristics of students enrolled and their outcomes. This focus will undoubtedly be a challenge for colleges and states that face numerous limitations in their data collection on noncredit, including its nonstandard format and wide range of students who may be reluctant to report data. However, several states in the study reported efforts to increase their data on noncredit students by improving noncredit reporting or making reporting a requirement. With the increased growth and importance of noncredit, it is likely that other states will follow suit and prompt colleges to develop better systems and methods to collect these data. The growth and prevalence of funding and programs, as well as the impetus toward greater accountability, point to a need for a better understanding of specific programs and student needs and experiences.

References

Alssid, J., and others. *Building a Career Pathways System: Promising Practices in Community College-Centered Workforce Development*. New York: Workforce Strategy Center, 2002.

Bailey, T. R., and others. *The Characteristics of Occupational Sub-Baccalaureate Students Entering the New Millennium*. New York: Columbia University, Teachers College, Community College Research Center, 2003.

Boswell, K. *State Funding for Community Colleges: A 50 State Survey*. Denver: Education Commission of the States, Center for Community College Policy, 2000.

Dougherty, K., and Bakia, M. *The New Economic Development Role of the Community College*. New York: Columbia University, Teachers College, Community College Research Center, 1999.

Jacobs, J., and Dougherty, K. "The Uncertain Future of the Community College Workforce Development Mission." In B. K. Townsend, K. J. Dougherty (eds.), *Community College Missions in the 21st Century*. New Directions for Community Colleges, No. 136. San Francisco: Jossey-Bass, 2006.

Leibowitz, M., and Taylor, J. C. "Breaking Through: Helping Low Skilled Adults Enter and Succeed in College and Careers." Boston: Jobs for the Future, 2004.

Morest, V. S. "Double Vision: How the Attempt to Balance Multiple Missions Is Shaping the Future of Community Colleges." In T. Bailey and V. S. Morest (eds.), *Defending the Community College Equity Agenda*. Baltimore, Md.: Johns Hopkins University Press, 2006.

Simon, M. *A Comprehensive Look at State-Funded, Employer-Focused Job Training Programs*. Washington, D.C.: National Governors Association, 1999.

U.S. Government Accountability Office. *Public Community Colleges and Technical Schools: Most Schools Use Credit and Noncredit Programs for Workforce Development*. Washington, D.C.: Government Accountability Office, 2004.

Van Noy, M., and others. *The Landscape of Noncredit Workforce Education: State Policies and Community College Practices*. New York: Columbia University, Teachers College, Community College Research Center, 2008.

Voorhees, R. A., and Milam, J. H. *The Hidden College: Noncredit Education in the United States*. Winchester, Va.: HigherEd.org, 2005.

Warford, L. J. "Funding Lifelong Learning: A National Priority." *Community College Journal*, 2002, 72(3), 15–18.

MICHELLE VAN NOY *is a senior research assistant at the Community College Research Center at Teachers College, Columbia University.*

JAMES JACOBS *is president of Macomb Community College in Warren, Michigan, and former associate director for community college operations at the Community College Research Center at Teachers College, Columbia University.*

10

Using California as a case study, this chapter provides new evidence on whether community colleges supply occupational training that meets the skill requirements of local employers.

How Well Do Community Colleges Respond to the Occupational Training Needs of Local Communities? Evidence from California

Duane E. Leigh, Andrew M. Gill

Rapid technological change and the relentless pressure exerted by global competition mean that job opportunities continuously appear in growing sectors of the economy and decline in stagnant sectors. The challenge for policymakers is to provide an educational and training system targeted to employment opportunities. Community colleges are widely viewed as the principal institutions within the U.S. system of higher education that provide adult training services. As community-based institutions, they are expected to be especially sensitive to local labor market conditions. Nevertheless, relatively little is known about their success in meeting changing local labor market needs. Using data for community colleges in the huge California Community College System (CCCS), this chapter asks how well community colleges are doing in supplying training that meets the skill requirements of local employers in a dynamic and ever-changing economy.

Existing Evidence

A fragmented literature examines the effectiveness of community colleges in responding to local employment needs. We view these studies as falling

We gratefully acknowledge the financial support of the W. E. Upjohn Institute for Employment Research.

into three categories. In the first are studies, such as those by Kane and Rouse (1995) and Leigh and Gill (1997), that use national data to show that community college programs substantially enhance labor market earnings prospects. But while evidence of positive average college earning effects is encouraging, Grubb (1996) makes the point that because occupational skills tend to be job specific, more credible evidence requires information specific to fields of study in community colleges and to geographical areas more closely aligned to local labor markets. Important studies that meet these criteria are Jacobson, LaLonde, and Sullivan's (2005a, 2005b) examinations of student records for displaced workers in Washington State matched to unemployment insurance earnings histories. Their most noteworthy finding is that earnings estimates differ substantially by major field of study. For men, large long-term quarterly earnings gains of about 14 percent are obtained for academic courses in science and mathematics, as well as for more technically oriented occupational skills, including courses in health occupations. The gains are larger for women—about 29 percent. For all other community college courses, long-term earnings gains for both males and females are close to zero. Unfortunately, there are few other available studies that use matched state administrative data sets to estimate returns to fields of study.

A second category of evidence is based on site visits to individual community college campuses. A leading example of this type of study is the large-scale U.S. Department of Education Community College Labor Market Responsiveness Initiative (MacAllum and Yoder, 2004). The initiative's main research output is a three-volume handbook designed to assist community colleges that wish to offer more market-driven curriculum. Drawing on information gained from site visits to more than 310 community colleges serving ten widely scattered labor market areas, the handbook develops seven modules summarizing important lessons learned. The first three relate to a college's internal leadership and governance, and the remaining four concern external relationships with funding sources, local employers, and other educational institutions.

The third category of evidence is specific to community college contract training. Contract training programs differ from regular community college curricula in that courses are tailored to meet the training requirements of particular employers. While virtually all colleges provide contract training to local employers, Dougherty (2003) shows that the level of contract training activity varies with the size and industry mix of local employers. In particular, large employers and firms in durable goods manufacturing and finance, insurance, and real estate are especially likely to use colleges' contract training programs. Isbell, Trutko, and Barnow (2000) make it clear that contract training pays off for trained workers in a number of ways, including high placement rates and hourly wages that exceed local averages. Unfortunately, data measuring contract training are limited and difficult to obtain. As Jacobson, Yudd, Feldman, and Petta (2005) pointed out, contract training seldom shows up in most colleges' data systems, which are geared to counting enrollment in for-credit courses to meet federal, state, and local reporting requirements.

Methodology and Data

What follows is a nontechnical presentation of a larger study done under a grant from the W. E. Upjohn Institute for Employment Research (Leigh and Gill, 2007). In this study, our objective was to move beyond the anecdotes provided by site visits to selected campuses, such as those carried out in the Department of Education initiative, to supply evidence of labor-market responsiveness based on data for the CCCS. The new approach we take builds on the preliminary analysis of Jacobson, Yudd, Feldman, and Petta (2005), which assesses the quality of matches between the supply and demand for training services at the local labor market level. Beginning with supply, we use CCCS student records to assign to each course completed a single occupational taxonomy of programs (TOP) code. Our primary data source is student records supplied by the CCCS Chancellor's Office for the 1996 cohort of first-time freshmen (FTF) attending 106 CCCS campuses. For each college, we use data on courses completed to calculate the percentage distribution of new skills learned by major occupational categories for a student cohort followed over six years. (The major occupational categories are listed in Table 10.2.)

On the demand side, we estimate demand for skills at the county level for the same major occupational TOP code categories. Demand-side measures come from occupational labor market-demand projections made, in cooperation with the CCCS Chancellor's Office, by the Labor Market Information Division of California's Employment Development Department. These projections are available for thirty-one California counties and four multicounty consortia, each of which contains several lightly populated counties. Projections are for the 1999–2006 period and include both replacement needs and net new jobs.

Using these measures of occupational labor supply and demand, we construct a measure of responsiveness (R) that indicates how closely the distribution of new skills supplied by each community college is matched with the distribution of projected new jobs in the county in which the college is located. A higher value of R indicates greater similarity between student training and projected new jobs, and hence a higher level of college responsiveness. (The equation and a complete explanation of our R measure may be found in Leigh and Gill, 2007.)

Results

The full results of this empirical study are too detailed to present here, but a brief summary in tabular form is presented as follows.

New Directions for Community Colleges • DOI: 10.1002/cc

Table 10.1. Responsiveness Values for California Community Colleges

Level of Aggregation	Mean	Maximum	Minimum
All 106 colleges	60.1	81.7	32.4
All 71 CC districts	62.3	82.1	42.5

Match Quality. The 106 community colleges in our data set are organized administratively into seventy-one districts. Most rural communities are served by a single community college that comprises its own district. In urban areas, districts may also be single-campus districts, but often they consist of more than one campus. In multicampus districts, member colleges may choose to coordinate their occupational curriculums in order to increase districtwide labor market responsiveness. If this is the case, the proper level for evaluating responsiveness is the district rather than the individual college.

By College. Table 10.1 presents R values at the college level calculated over ten major occupational categories for which we have data for all thirty-five counties and consortia.

The (unweighted) average value of R over all 106 colleges in our data set is 60.1 percent, with a substantial range between maximum and minimum estimates of 49.3 percentage points. The maximum R value of 81.7 percent is obtained for Mission College located in Santa Clara County just west of the city of San Jose in northern California; the minimum value of 32.4 percent is for East Los Angeles College (ELAC) in southern California. Remember, a high R value indicates that the college or district is more responsive to the demands of the local labor market.

Table 10.2 goes into detail on the quality of the matches calculated for Mission College and ELAC. The table shows that Mission College comes very close to matching the shares of projected new jobs in Santa Clara County in business and engineering technology, the two fields of study with the largest shares of projected new jobs (32.4 percent and 21.7 percent, respectively). Notice also that Mission College's supply of credits completed in information technology closely matches Santa Clara County's demand in this field (9.5 percent). Only for "other services" does supply fail to closely match demand.

At ELAC, new credits completed consistently fall short of projected demand for Los Angeles County. The one exception to this statement is "other services," where added supply greatly exceeds projected demand for the county. "Other services" is a highly aggregated occupational category that includes community services, paralegal, and education services such as special education aide. A closer look at data for ELAC reveals that student

Table 10.2. Comparison by Major Occupation of Labor Demand and Supply for Mission College and East Los Angeles College (percentages)

	Mission College		East Los Angeles College	
Occupation	Supply	Demand	Supply	Demand
Agriculture technology	0.3%	1.5%	0.0%	1.6%
Business	27.6	32.4	11.2	36.2
Information technology	11.8	9.5	6.3	2.5
Engineering technology	26.3	21.7	3.4	16.2
Construction crafts	0.0	3.8	0.0	3.2
Health care	12.5	10.5	4.5	13.0
Fashion and child development	1.7	0.5	13.5	1.3
Food and hospitality	5.3	9.5	0.5	12.4
Commercial services	0.0	4.2	0.0	4.7
Other services	14.4	6.3	60.5	9.0

credits completed are heavily concentrated within other services in the detailed administration of justice TOP code category. The college's Web site notes that ELAC is well known for training criminal justice system personnel and that it maintains a special relationship with criminal justice agencies, including the Los Angeles County Sheriff's Department. Since ELAC is a member of the nine-campus Los Angeles Community College District, this case illustrates the possibility that even a college that seems unresponsive according to our methodology may be offering a specialized occupational curriculum that complements those offered by other colleges in its district.

By District. Leigh and Gill (2007) indicate that all of the lowest-scoring (least-responsive) colleges in our data set are members of multicampus districts. Because district R scores are a weighted average of member college scores, we would expect to find, as shown in the second row of Table 10.1, that the minimum R score at the district level is substantially higher (10.1 percentage points) than the minimum R for colleges. At the other extreme, however, we report the unexpected result that the maximum district R score of 82.1 percent is slightly higher, rather than lower, than the maximum college score of 81.7 percent.

In Leigh and Gill (2007), we explore the data for cases in which district R scores exceed those for member colleges. A leading example is the San Mateo County Community College District for which we report the highest R score shown in Table 10.1 (82.1 percent). This district comprises three community colleges, all of which have lower R scores than that of the district. (R scores of member community colleges are 76.9 percent, 75.0 percent, and

56.2 percent.) Our interpretation is that in these districts, member colleges offer complementary curriculum specializations so that the district, rather than the individual member colleges, is labor market responsive.

This evidence is consistent with conversations with Willard Hom, director of the research and planning unit in the CCCS Chancellor's Office, that indicates that multicampus districts vary greatly in the extent of their intercollege curriculum coordination. He explains that in some districts, districtwide curriculum committees exercise considerable direct control over the curriculum committees of individual member campuses. In other districts, the district committee serves a coordinating and information-sharing function rather than an approval function. Still other districts have no districtwide curriculum committee at all.

Regression Findings. In the second part of our analysis, we used multivariate regression to attempt to explain differences in match quality across colleges and districts. Space limits our ability to go into detail on our results. However, one interesting finding is that a college's emphasis on occupational curricula does not necessarily make it responsive to the local labor market. Drawing on the discussion of Jacobson, Yudd, Feldman, and Petta (2005), we also assess the impact on responsiveness of measures of fiscal capacity: enrollment, district revenue per students, and district local revenue share. Our results indicate that these measures have the anticipated positive sign and are statistically significant but that the magnitudes of their effects are not large.

Probably our most striking regression result is that, controlling for the effect of fiscal capacity variables, multicampus districts report R scores nearly 6 percentage points higher than those for single-campus districts. Based on the commonsense property of a weighted average, a reasonable expectation for districts is that the effect of the multicampus variable should be about zero. The reason is that downward pressure on the R scores of multicampus districts including high-scoring colleges would be just offset by upward pressure on R scores for multicampus districts including low-scoring colleges. Our finding of a positive multicampus effect suggests that complementary (coordinated) curriculum planning by multicampus districts makes them more responsive.

Conclusion

This chapter has provided a brief nontechnical overview of an empirical study of the labor market responsiveness of California community colleges. Although it is hazardous to generalize from results for one state, we believe that our findings should be of interest to researchers and policymakers concerned with higher education issues in other states. We have three major findings:

Colleges that offer a high proportion of vocational courses or credits are not necessarily better at responding to local needs. Those that offer fewer options that are more targeted may do just as well.

Higher levels of local funding are positively associated with responsiveness, but the connection is a loose one. We find plenty of room for college administrators to exercise initiative in seizing opportunities offered in their communities. Leadership can make a difference.

A low score on our responsiveness measure for a college that is part of a multicampus district may simply reflect coordination at the district level to offer a cost-effective mix of occupational programs. In this case, the district rather than the individual college is the proper unit for judging labor market responsiveness. This has implications for measuring institutional effectiveness.

Based on the results of our quantitative study, we find little to contradict the conclusions of qualitative studies of the same issue: market-responsive colleges have leaderships that are committed to a market-responsive mission, have an internal response mechanism dedicated to rapidly developing new occupational skills curricula, and have close ties to local employers and workforce and educational organizations. Those seeking a more detailed discussion of these issues, as well as an examination of whether California community colleges are meeting the needs of their immigrant populations, are referred to the larger study from which this chapter is drawn (Leigh and Gill, 2007).

References

Dougherty, K. J. "The Uneven Distribution of Employee Training by Community Colleges: Description and Explanation." *Annals of the American Academy of Political and Social Science,* 2003, *586*(1), 62–91.

Grubb. W. N. *Working in the Middle: Strengthening Education and Training for the Mid-Skilled Labor Force.* San Francisco: Jossey-Bass, 1996.

Isbell, K., Trutko, J., and Barnow, B. S. "Customized Training for Employers: Training People for Jobs That Exist and Employers Who Want to Hire Them." In B. S. Barnow and C. T. Kings (eds.), *Improving the Odds: Increasing the Effectiveness of Publicly Funded Training.* Washington, D.C.: Urban Institute Press, 2000.

Jacobson, L., LaLonde, R. J., and Sullivan, D. "The Impact of Community College Retraining on Older Displaced Workers: Should We Teach Old Dogs New Tricks?" *Industrial and Labor Relations Review,* 2005a, *58*(3), 398–415.

Jacobson, L., LaLonde, R. J., and Sullivan, D. "Estimating the Returns to Community College Schooling for Displaced Workers." *Journal of Econometrics,* 2005b, *125*(1–2), 271–304.

Jacobson, L., Yudd, R., Feldman, L., and Petta, I. *The 21st-Century Community College: A Strategic Guide for Maximizing Labor Market Responsiveness, Research Appendices.* Washington, D.C.: U.S. Department of Education, Office of Vocational and Adult Education, 2005.

Kane, T. J., and Rouse, E. R. "Labor-Market Returns to Two- and Four-Year College." *American Economic Review,* 1995, *85*(3), 600–614.

Leigh, D. E., and Gill, A. M. "Labor Market Returns to Community Colleges: Evidence for Returning Adults." *Journal of Human Resources,* 1997, *32*(4), 334–353.

Leigh, D. E., and Gill, A. M. *Do Community Colleges Respond to Local Needs? Evidence from California.* Kalamazoo, Mich.: W. E. Upjohn Institute for Employment Research, 2007.

MacAllum, K., and Yoder, K. *The 21st-Century Community College: A Strategic Guide for Maximizing Labor Market Responsiveness.* Washington, D.C.: U.S. Department of Education, Office of Vocational and Adult Education, 2004.

DUANE E. LEIGH *is professor emeritus of economics at Washington State University, Pullman.*

ANDREW M. GILL *is professor of economics at California State University Fullerton.*

11

State-level interest in meeting workforce needs and facilitating adults' baccalaureate attainment is changing conceptions of the applied associate degree and the mission of the community college.

The Outlook for Transfer Programs and the Direction of the Community College

Barbara K. Townsend

Employment projections made by the U.S. Bureau of Labor Statistics (BLS) show that most of the high-wage jobs of the future will require a bachelor's degree or higher for entry-level positions or for job advancement (Dohm and Shniper, 2007). Other chapters in this volume have echoed the same theme and have suggested that perhaps more students entering the community college ought to be guided into pathways that will allow easy transfer into baccalaureate programs.

With the economic returns to education growing, talk of impending labor shortages in critical technical and professional areas has become common. Accordingly, some have emphasized the important contribution that community colleges can make in increasing the nation's output of graduates with bachelor's degrees (U.S. Department of Education, 2006). Certainly more can be done to smooth the transition from the two-year to the four-year college for students who desire a bachelor's degree. However, given the funding and campus obstacles to expanding the more expensive seats in public four-year colleges, several states are attempting to meet the demand for more bachelor's degrees by allowing community colleges to expand their mission and offer the degree.

Critics of the community college have agued that the higher-level skills necessary for most high-wage jobs are not developed in terminal occupational programs (Brint and Karabel, 1989; Dougherty, 1994). These skills

New Directions for Community Colleges, no. 146, Summer 2009 © 2009 Wiley Periodicals, Inc.
Published online in Wiley InterScience (www.interscience.wiley.com) • DOI: 10.1002/cc.371

are supposedly provided in the associate of arts (A.A.) degree, also called the transfer degree, but not sufficiently provided in the applied programs that lead to the associate of applied science degree (A.A.S.) in some states or the associate of science (A.S.) degree in states without the A.A.S. degree. Since the A.S. degree in some states is also considered a transfer degree, albeit one oriented to the sciences, I shall use the A.A.S. degree in the rest of this chapter to represent applied associate programs. The A.A.S. degree is considered terminal because it "consist[s] of occupational or technical courses that are not required and thus are not transferable into conventional academic baccalaureate degrees" (Arney, Hardebeck, Estrada, and Permenter, 2006, p. 186).

Although the criticism of the community college for tracking students into essentially dead-end jobs through its occupational programs may have been valid in the past, this view of the community college does not acknowledge the emerging phenomenon of the applied baccalaureate. The applied baccalaureate is a bachelor's degree designed to incorporate applied associate courses and degrees once considered as terminal while providing students with the higher-order thinking skills so desired in today's job market. When offered by a four-year college or university, the applied baccalaureate has been defined as a "baccalaureate program designed to meet the needs of nontraditional students by allowing technical hours to be transferred for credit to a baccalaureate degree" (Arney, Hardeveck, Estrada, and Permenter, 2006, p. 184). Typically this degree is titled bachelor of applied science (B.A.S.), but it may have other titles, such as bachelor of science technology (B.S.T.), bachelor of technology (B.T.), or bachelor of applied arts and sciences (B.A.A.S.).

In this chapter, I draw on data from a recent study about the applied baccalaureate degree (Townsend and Bragg, 2008) to describe the growing presence in public higher education of this degree. Sometimes the applied baccalaureate is offered by the community college and sometimes by the four-year college. I describe the applied baccalaureate in more detail, then discuss its appearance in four-year colleges and in two-year institutions, and conclude with an assessment of its impact on higher education in general, as well as on the community college's transfer mission and overall mission or place in academe.

The Applied Baccalaureate Degree

The typical U.S. baccalaureate degree consists of three components: general education courses, electives, and courses in one's major or intended area of specialization or concentration. General education courses are typically taken in the first two years to provide some of the skills necessary for upper-division work and to provide exposure to various fields so that the student can decide on a major (Alexander, 1993). Courses in one's major are generally taken in the junior and senior years and are considered upper-division courses. Electives can be taken throughout the degree program.

NEW DIRECTIONS FOR COMMUNITY COLLEGES • DOI: 10.1002/cc

In contrast to this traditional baccalaureate, some two-year and four-year schools have developed an applied baccalaureate degree in which the bulk of a student's major or area of specialization is taken during the first two years of study, as the person completes the applied associate degree. Additional general education courses sufficient to meet the four-year program's general education requirements are taken in the student's junior and senior years.

There are other differences between the applied baccalaureate and the traditional baccalaureate. According to Walker and Floyd (2005), the "applied baccalaureate is different from the traditional baccalaureate in that the former uses applied and contextual learning methods, and significant learning on the job, while the latter depends principally on academic pedagogy" (p. 95). They also assert that the applied baccalaureate programs "have been specifically created to meet identified workforce demands such as teacher education and certification, nursing, culinary arts, electronics technology, information systems technology, computing and business administration" (p. 95). Other applied fields are automotive technology management, criminal justice, drafting, food service, and industrial technology.

States are supporting the development of the applied baccalaureate as a means to provide greater access to the baccalaureate, especially for adult learners, defined as individuals twenty-four and older (Donaldson and Townsend, 2007) who are in the job market or workforce but lack baccalaureate credentials. According to a recent national report on adult learning (Council for Adult and Experiential Learning, 2008), approximately 20 percent of adults have some college education but have not attained a degree. The percentage of this group varies by state, with Alaska having the highest percentage (27.5) and Massachusetts the lowest (15.5).

The applied baccalaureate is also justified as workforce development. Bragg (2001) and others have identified the applied baccalaureate as a logical extension of career pathway curricula that emphasize initial entry into the community college and extend the educational pathway to four-year applied baccalaureate degree programs. These programs are cited as models for enhancing workforce and economic development (Ignash and Kotun, 2005) and are receiving support from various sources, including the U.S. Department of Education and foundations such as Charles Stewart Mott and Joyce, to expand implementation in the United States.

Four-Year College Applied Baccalaureate

In the public sector of higher education, the majority of states (thirty-eight) offer the applied baccalaureate. Sometimes this degree is offered in both the two-year and four-year sector. However, over half the states permit only four-year colleges to award the applied baccalaureate degree. These states include Arizona, Arkansas, Kansas, Kentucky, Missouri, Ohio, Oklahoma, Pennsylvania, South Dakota, and Tennessee. Currently, four of these states

(Arizona, Illinois, Michigan, and Wisconsin) are considering permitting two-year colleges to award the baccalaureate, which may or may not be restricted to the applied baccalaureate.

Oklahoma is an example of a state with numerous four-year public institutions offering the applied baccalaureate. Two institutions (Cameron University and Langston University) were authorized before 1991 to award the bachelor of science technology (B.S.T.) degree, designed to build on associate degree technology programs and prepare graduates with this credential for supervisory or middle-management positions. Also, before 1991, Oklahoma Panhandle State University was authorized to award the bachelor of technology (B.T.) and the bachelor of international business management (B.I.B.M.), with both degrees designed for students with technical backgrounds. Since 1991, eight more four-year public colleges have been authorized to award an applied baccalaureate, which is always designed to articulate with an A.A.S. degree. The baccalaureates include not only the B.T. but also the bachelor of applied arts and sciences (B.A.A.S.).

The University of Hawaii system is trying to find ways to allow adult learners with some college credits to come back to college and get what they need, whether it be a degree or further training. The impetus behind this effort is a shortage of educated people for the workforce. Thus, the system is seeking ways of continuing links with its community colleges and four-year institutions by building programs for associate degree recipients. As an example, the University of West O'ahu has recently been authorized to award a B.A.S. in respiratory therapy. The program at the university works as a management top to a two-year college associate degree in respiratory therapy.

Texas not only permits selected two-year colleges to offer an applied baccalaureate but also has twenty public four-year schools that have a bachelor of applied arts and sciences (B.A.A.S.) program. In addition, the University of Texas at Brownsville offers the bachelor of applied technology (B.A.T.). There are several reasons that the applied baccalaureate is so available in Texas. First, the state has 3 million adults who have some college credit but no baccalaureate. The applied baccalaureate is seen as a degree that appeals primarily to adults. Also, the state's strategic plan for higher education, Closing the Gap, has set high target rates for baccalaureate completion of various demographic groups. The applied baccalaureate is seen as a way to help meet the target rates. Also, some of the four-year institutions, such as Texas A&M, Kingsville, and University of Texas at Brownsville, have land grant connections that make them interested in the applied baccalaureate.

The Community College Baccalaureate

Not only the four-year college but also the community college may offer an applied baccalaureate. When the community college does so, the degree is commonly referred to as a "community college baccalaureate" (Floyd, Skolnik, and Walker, 2005). This phrase is somewhat problematic because it sug-

NEW DIRECTIONS FOR COMMUNITY COLLEGES • DOI: 10.1002/cc

gests that a baccalaureate awarded by a community college is somehow different from the baccalaureate awarded by a four-year college (Twombly, 2005). However, I will use the phrase since it is so commonly accepted to describe a baccalaureate offered and awarded by a two-year college. At least thirteen states have authorized one or more of their community colleges to award the baccalaureate degree. In so doing, some have specified that the community college may offer a baccalaureate in only a very specific applied area while other states permit a wider range of two-year college baccalaureate offerings.

States that currently limit the kind of baccalaureate degrees community colleges may offer include North Dakota and Texas. Thus, Bismarck State College, a two-year institution in North Dakota, has recently been authorized to develop an online B.A.S. in a specific applied field: energy management. To enter the program, students need to have earned an A.A.S. in one of Bismarck State College's energy education programs. Texas legislation permits community colleges to offer only baccalaureates in applied science and technology. Currently three Texas community colleges offer these kinds of baccalaureates. In fall 2005, Brazosport College began offering the B.A.T. degree, which has four specialty areas: process operations management; safety, health, and environmental management; business management; and general technology management. Midland College also offers the B.A.T., with a major in organizational management. This 126-hour degree is built on an A.A.S. degree in one of five areas. South Texas College has two bachelor degree programs: the B.A.T. in technology management and the B.A.T. in computer and information technology.

Other states have permitted one or more community colleges to offer a wider range of baccalaureate programs partly because of severe workforce shortages in certain areas, particularly in teaching and nursing. Largely for this reason, in 2001 Florida authorized selected community colleges to award the baccalaureate degree in an applied area of study, including education and nursing. In 2007 the legislature authorized all community colleges in Florida to submit a proposal to offer a baccalaureate degree, which may or may not be an applied baccalaureate. At the time of the writing of this chapter, ten institutions had been authorized to award the baccalaureate. St. Petersburg College, formerly St. Petersburg Junior College, has led the state in developing baccalaureate programs; as of June 2008, it offers twenty baccalaureate programs, including nine in various areas of teacher education.

The latest development in Florida's authorization of baccalaureates in community colleges is legislation to create the Florida College System, which will comprise former community colleges that had been authorized to develop and award "baccalaureate degree programs that are designed to meet regional and statewide employment needs" (Florida Senate Bill 1716, 2008). In June 2008 the governor signed this legislation, and the system is now being developed.

Florida is not the only state where a shift in institutional type is being dictated at the state level. The Georgia Board of Regents, on behalf of the

NEW DIRECTIONS FOR COMMUNITY COLLEGES • DOI: 10.1002/cc

University System of Georgia, has authorized several of its thirteen two-year colleges to award the baccalaureate. When this occurs, the institution becomes a state college. Thus Georgia, like Florida, is creating a system of state colleges where none previously existed.

In other states, the change from two-year to four-year status happens institution by institution rather than as part of a state-level decision to automatically change all community colleges awarding a baccalaureate to a four-year college. For example, on an institution-by-institution basis, two of Utah's community colleges have become four-year schools. What is now called Dixie State College of Utah has roots reaching back to 1911. In 2000 it was granted four-year status and received permission to offer a few four-year degrees. As of 2007–2008 it offers eight baccalaureate programs, including a B.A. and B.S. in English, a B.S.N. in nursing, and a B.S. in elementary education. Utah Valley State College, which began as Central Utah Vocational School in 1941, was granted the authority to award the baccalaureate degree in 1993. Effective July 1, 2008, it was renamed Utah State University and was authorized to award a master's of education degree, with the promise of more master's degrees to follow.

Conclusion

Over the past few decades higher education has changed from being the purview of the elite—people with the time, money, desire, and academic ability to spend several years in full-time study—to being a prerequisite for the higher-level jobs in the modern economy. Prompted by the 1947 Truman Commission Report, the community college has been a major force in expanding higher education to large underserved segments of the population. In a growing number of states, it is now being called on to take on the job of increasing the baccalaureate production rate, particularly among adults, with little increase in the institutional infrastructure. The goal is to produce a more educated (or at least more highly credentialed) workforce at a lower cost. Whether the applied baccalaureate will help close the education gap in the United States is an open question. Will employers accept it as meeting the requirements for the high-wage jobs of the future? How will graduate schools treat the degree for students wishing to study for more advanced degrees? Will the applied baccalaureate become the newest addition to the educational tracking system and be subject to the same type of criticism that the community college occupational programs once were? Only time will tell.

However, at the conceptual level, this relatively new degree is controversial for several reasons. One reason is that it calls into question the role of general education in a baccalaureate. Typically placed in the first two years of the degree, it is required partly to introduce students to the various disciplines in which they could major. General education is also designed partly to prepare students for upper-division work by providing them with appropriate knowledge and skills.

Another problematic aspect of the applied baccalaureate is that it blurs the lines between upper-division and lower-division courses. In theory, major courses are primarily taken in the junior and senior years as upper-division courses because they rest on the broad foundation of knowledge and skills provided by general education. The applied baccalaureate degree may call this theory into question, for when major courses are taken in the first two years of a bachelor's degree, they rarely require much, if any, of the knowledge and skills learned in general education courses. An applied baccalaureate clearly equals four years of college-level work and credits. What is less clear is whether the degree equals four years of progressively difficult college-level work where the courses build on each other sequentially. Independent of this issue is another one that affects students: with this degree, students lack the curricular flexibility to take electives in areas of interest. There is choice for general education electives, but none beyond that.

Regardless of what some view as problematic curricular dimensions of the applied baccalaureate, its existence is changing the community college in at least two ways. One way is that the institution's transfer function should no longer be thought of just in terms of the A.A. degree. An applied associate degree will now transfer in more than thirty-five states where at least one of their public four-year schools offers the applied baccalaureate. The applied associate degree can now be viewed as the foundation of a four-year applied baccalaureate degree, designed to incorporate transferred A.A.S. courses and degrees.

Another way the applied baccalaureate is changing the community college is by changing its position in the hierarchy of higher education institutions. Once a community college offers a baccalaureate degree, one must ask whether it can still be considered a two-year school. Some states, such as Georgia and Florida, are answering that question in the negative by changing these institutions into four-year state colleges. The Carnegie Foundation has also developed some new basic categories or labels for institutions whose primary program offerings are associate degrees and certificates but also have one or more baccalaureate programs. One category is "baccalaureate/associate's colleges," a category first used in the foundation's 2000 classification system. To be in this category, at least 10 percent but no more than 50 percent of an institution's degrees awarded annually must be baccalaureates. Another category is "associate's dominant." First presented in the 2005 classification system, this category means that the percentage of baccalaureate degrees awarded annually is less than 20 percent.

The extent to which the applied baccalaureate will facilitate baccalaureate attainment by adult learners and provide a more skilled workforce is unclear. Few states are collecting data on this degree, partly because it is a recent curricular offering in many of the states that now offer it. It is important to monitor both the extent of this degree and its efficacy in increasing baccalaureate attainment and a skilled workforce. Leaders of the community college, in particular, have a vested interest in this monitoring since the

NEW DIRECTIONS FOR COMMUNITY COLLEGES • DOI: 10.1002/cc

applied baccalaureate has great potential for extending the community college's transfer mission and realigning the community college within the hierarchy of higher education institutions.

References

Alexander, J. C. "The Irrational Disciplinarity of Undergraduate Education." *Chronicle of Higher Education,* Dec. 1, 1993, p. B3.

Arney, J. B., Hardebeck, S., Estrada, J., and Permenter, V. "An Innovative Baccalaureate Degree: Applied Versus Traditional." *Journal of Hispanic Higher Education,* 2006, 5(2), 184–194.

Bragg, D. D. "Opportunities and Challenges for the New Vocationalism." In D. D. Bragg (ed.), *The New Vocationalism in American Community Colleges.* New Directions for Community Colleges, no. 115. San Francisco: Jossey-Bass, 2001.

Brint, S., and Karabel, J. *The Diverted Dream.* New York: Oxford University Press, 1989.

Council for Adult and Experiential Learning. *Adult Learning in Focus: National and State-by-State Data.* 2008. Chicago: Author.

Dohm, A., and Shniper, L. "Occupational Employment Projections to 2016." *Monthly Labor Review,* 2007, *130*(11), 86–125.

Donaldson, J., and Townsend, B. K. "Higher Education Journals' Discourse About Adult Undergraduate Students." *Journal of Higher Education,* 2007, 78(1), 27–50.

Dougherty, K. J. *The Contradictory College.* Albany: State University of New York Press, 1994.

Florida. Senate Bill 1716. 2008. Accessed June 16, 2008, at http://www.flsenate.gov.

Floyd, D., Skolnik, M., and Walker, K. *Community College Baccalaureate: Emerging Trends and Policy Issues.* Sterling, Va.: Stylus Publishing, 2005.

Ignash, J., and Kotun, D. "Results of a National Study of Transfer in Occupational/Technical Degrees: Policies and Practices." *Journal of Applied Research in the Community College,* 2005, *12*(2), 109–12.

Townsend, B. K., and Bragg, D. *The Adult Learner and the Applied Baccalaureate.* Indianapolis, Ind.: Lumina Foundation for Education, 2008.

Twombly, S. "Review of *The Community College Baccalaureate.*" *Journal of Applied Research in Community Colleges,* 2005, *13*(1), 93–95.

U.S. Department of Education. *A Test of Leadership: Charting the Future of U.S. Higher Education.* Washington, D.C.: U.S. Government Printing Office, 2006.

Utah Valley State College. "Mission Statement Effective 12.14.07." 2007. Accessed June 14, 2008, at http://www.usvc.edu/visitors/aboutusvc/mission.html.

Walker, K. P., and Floyd, D. L. "Applied and Workforce Baccalaureates." In D. Floyd, M. Skolnik, and K. Walker (eds.), *Community College Baccalaureate: Emerging Trends and Policy Issues.* Sterling, Va.: Stylus Publishing, 2005.

BARBARA K. TOWNSEND *is professor of higher education and director of the Center for Community College Research at the University of Missouri.*

INDEX